Getting Started with OpenCart Module Development

Master your OpenCart modules and code!

Rupak Nepali

[PACKT] open source *
PUBLISHING   community experience distilled

BIRMINGHAM - MUMBAI

Getting Started with OpenCart Module Development

First published: October 2013

Production Reference: 1211013

Published by Packt Publishing Ltd.

Livery Place
35 Livery Street
Birmingham B3 2PB, UK.

ISBN 978-1-78328-037-7

www.packtpub.com

Cover Image by Aniket Sawant (aniket_sawant_photography@hotmail.com)

Credits

Author
Rupak Nepali

Reviewers
Jack W. Davis
Aditya Menon

Acquisition Editor
Akram Hussain

Commissioning Editor
Subho Gupta

Technical Editors
Pooja Arondekar
Menza Mathew

Copy Editor
Mradula Hegde
Sayanee Mukherjee

Project Coordinator
Amey Sawant

Proofreader
Bernadette Watkins

Indexer
Monica Ajmera Mehta

Production Coordinator
Adonia Jones

Cover Work
Adonia Jones

About the Author

Rupak Nepali, a PHP programmer from Nepal, has been working on OpenCart since 2010 and has completed many projects and made many modules on OpenCart to meet client requirements. He handles `http://opencartnepal.com` personally as well as updates his personal site `http://rupaknepali.com.np` with his works Mr. Nepali currently works as a full-time freelancer on oDesk as well as on various freelancer sites. He holds a Bachelor's degree in Computer Information Systems.

I wish to thank my parents, especially my mother Subthara Nepali and my father Bhairab Nepali, who emphasized the importance of literacy, and my brothers who helped at every step, as well as all my friends, and seniors, who provided their support and encouragement to write this book.

Thanks to Packt Publishing who provided me with such a great opportunity and all the team members who assisted me in publishing this book.

About the Reviewers

Jack W. Davis is an e-commerce developer specializing in OpenCart and on-page SEO for online stores. He runs an OpenCart development company called Destrove, which has helped hundreds of businesses expand, upgrade, and design their e-commerce stores. With years of development experience and a creative outlook on software design, Jack has become a recognized figure in OpenCart development communities.

Jack also runs a popular e-commerce news and tutorial website `www.CartAdvisor.com`, where he spends most of his time writing about e-commerce software and helping others customize their online stores.

Aditya Menon is an experienced developer, and the web is his primary platform. Aditya works for Adbhuth, a privately held start-up. An overview of his strengths, functions, and aspirations include predominantly using PHP and JavaScript. He has written and improvised applications working with teams from across five continents. He is happy to produce and extend intelligently built code bases, with exemplary architectures. He also follows industry standards and best practice discussions closely, and acts on wisdom gained from these arenas. Aditya is currently a consultant and a developer on multiple start-up teams from across the world. He is constantly on the lookout for new tools and techniques to make development faster, easier, and more joyful. He looks at a future where technology in general and software in particular, play even more important and impressive roles in human life. Learning new languages and paradigms to build these tools of the future is what delights him the most. He currently lives in New Delhi, India. He is a 23-year-old man, eager to travel the world, and explore new opportunities.

I would like to thank Mymo, mom, and dad!

www.PacktPub.com

Support files, eBooks, discount offers and more

You might want to visit www.PacktPub.com for support files and downloads related to your book.

Did you know that Packt offers eBook versions of every book published, with PDF and ePub files available? You can upgrade to the eBook version at www.PacktPub.com and as a print book customer, you are entitled to a discount on the eBook copy. Get in touch with us at service@packtpub.com for more details.

At www.PacktPub.com, you can also read a collection of free technical articles, sign up for a range of free newsletters and receive exclusive discounts and offers on Packt books and eBooks.

![PACKTLIB logo]

http://PacktLib.PacktPub.com

Do you need instant solutions to your IT questions? PacktLib is Packt's online digital book library. Here, you can access, read and search across Packt's entire library of books.

Why Subscribe?

- Fully searchable across every book published by Packt
- Copy and paste, print and bookmark content
- On demand and accessible via web browser

Free Access for Packt account holders

If you have an account with Packt at www.PacktPub.com, you can use this to access PacktLib today and view nine entirely free books. Simply use your login credentials for immediate access.

Table of Contents

Preface

If you can code OpenCart modules, you can customize OpenCart and make e-commerce sites easier to administer and also change the way the default OpenCart system works. This book shows you how to create all sorts of extensions: OpenCart module, Order Total module, ideas for creating payment, shipping modules, and ways to create custom pages and forms on OpenCart module to carry out the insert, edit, delete, and list functions.

This book focuses on teaching you all aspects of OpenCart modules by showing and defining code examples. The book uses default OpenCart module to clone other modules, the process by which one module gets transferred to another. It shows each and every line of code and describes them so readers know what the code does. You will clone the Google_talk module in the first chapter. In the second chapter, you will learn about all the available methods in OpenCart, and at last you will create two custom module feedback pages and the Tips Order Total modules.

Each chapter teaches you to make a new OpenCart module; you will thus be able to make three modules by reading this book. You will be able to create the Hello World module by cloning the Google talk module that you can then change to the Welcome Message module. Likewise, you will get a description of each code of default featured module of OpenCart, and then create the Feedback pages to manage the feedbacks. In the end, you will be able to create an Order Total module called Tips Order Total module.

Each chapter builds a practical module from the ground up using step-by-step instructions and examples.

What this book covers

Chapter 1, Getting Started with OpenCart Module, shows us how to clone the Google_talk module to the Hello World module and lists ways to install, configure, and uninstall the OpenCart module and show the structure of the file of admin and frontend.

Chapter 2, Describing The Code of Extensions, lists all global methods of OpenCart, shows you how to configure the feature module, describes the code of the feature module, shows the way to start the coding for the shipping module, and describes the payment module.

Chapter 3, Create Custom OpenCart Module, shows you how to create a feedback module and the Tips Order Total module. It also shows how code works and are managed.

What you need for this book

OpenCart, along with knowledge of the backend and frontend of the software is needed for this book.

Who this book is for

This book is for programmers working with OpenCart, who want to develop custom OpenCart modules. You need to be familiar with the basics of OpenCart and PHP programming; after reading the book, you will be able to create customized OpenCart modules.

Conventions

In this book, you will find a number of styles of text that distinguish between different kinds of information. Here are some examples of these styles, and an explanation of their meaning.

Code words in text are shown as follows: " As given at the controller, `$group=helloworld`, `$data` is `$_POST`, and `$store_id` is 0.."

A block of code is set as follows:

```
public function install($type, $code) {
  $this->db->query("INSERT INTO " . DB_PREFIX ."extension SET `type`
= '" . $this->db->escape($type) . "', `code` = '" . $this->db-
>escape($code) . "'");
}
```

New terms and **important words** are shown in bold. Words that you see on the screen, in menus or dialog boxes, for example, appear in the text like this: " The file structure is divided into two sections **admin** and **catalog**".

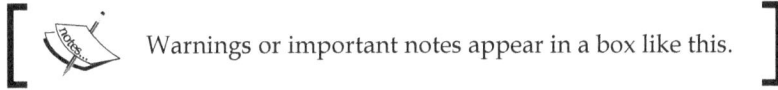

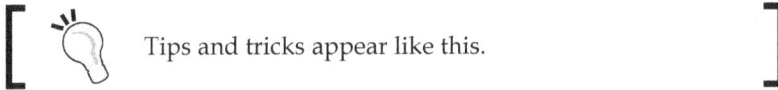

> Warnings or important notes appear in a box like this.

> Tips and tricks appear like this.

Reader feedback

Feedback from our readers is always welcome. Let us know what you think about this book—what you liked or may have disliked. Reader feedback is important for us to develop titles that you really get the most out of.

To send us general feedback, simply send an e-mail to feedback@packtpub.com, and mention the book title via the subject of your message.

If there is a topic that you have expertise in and you are interested in either writing or contributing to a book, see our author guide on www.packtpub.com/authors.

Customer support

Now that you are the proud owner of a Packt book, we have a number of things to help you to get the most from your purchase.

Downloading the example code

You can download the example code files for all Packt books you have purchased from your account at http://www.packtpub.com. If you purchased this book elsewhere, you can visit http://www.packtpub.com/support and register to have the files e-mailed directly to you.

Errata

Although we have taken every care to ensure the accuracy of our content, mistakes do happen. If you find a mistake in one of our books—maybe a mistake in the text or the code—we would be grateful if you would report this to us. By doing so, you can save other readers from frustration and help us improve subsequent versions of this book. If you find any errata, please report them by visiting http://www.packtpub.com/submit-errata, selecting your book, clicking on the **errata submission form** link, and entering the details of your errata. Once your errata are verified, your submission will be accepted and the errata will be uploaded on our website, or added to any list of existing errata, under the Errata section of that title. Any existing errata can be viewed by selecting your title from http://www.packtpub.com/support.

Piracy

Piracy of copyright material on the Internet is an ongoing problem across all media. At Packt, we take the protection of our copyright and licenses very seriously. If you come across any illegal copies of our works, in any form, on the Internet, please provide us with the location address or website name immediately so that we can pursue a remedy.

Please contact us at copyright@packtpub.com with a link to the suspected pirated material.

We appreciate your help in protecting our authors, and our ability to bring you valuable content.

Questions

You can contact us at questions@packtpub.com if you are having a problem with any aspect of the book, and we will do our best to address it.

1
Getting Started with OpenCart Modules

OpenCart is an e-commerce cart application built with its own in-house framework that uses the **Model View Controller** (**MVC**) language pattern; thus each module in OpenCart also follows the MVCL patterns. The controller creates logic and gathers data from the model and passes it to display them in the view. The OpenCart modules have `admin` and `catalog` folders. The files in the `admin` folder help in controlling the settings of modules and the files in the `catalog` folder handle the presentation layer (frontend). Each module has its own files by which it gets modular, and changing one module's file does not affect other modules.

Creating the Hello World module

We assume that you already know PHP and have installed OpenCart, and are familiar with the OpenCart backend and frontend, as well as you have some coding knowledge of PHP.

You are going to create the Hello World module which just has one input box in the admin settings for the module, and the same content is shown on the frontend. The first step to creating a module is using a unique name, so that there will not be a conflict with other modules. The same unique name is used to create the filename and classname to extend the controller and the model.

There are generally six to eight files that need to be created for each module, and they follow a similar structure. If there is an interaction with the database tables, we have to create two extra models. The following screenshot shows the hierarchy of files and folders of an OpenCart module:

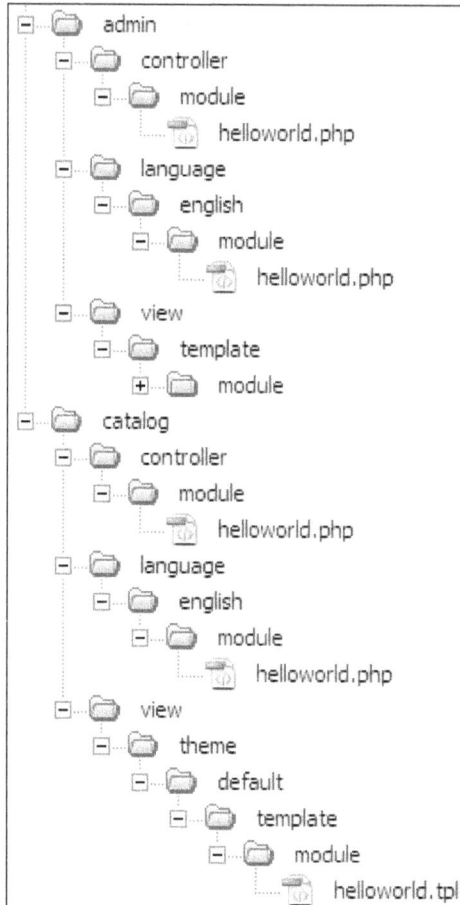

```
admin
   controller
      module
         helloworld.php
   language
      english
         module
            helloworld.php
   view
      template
         module
catalog
   controller
      module
         helloworld.php
   language
      english
         module
            helloworld.php
   view
      theme
         default
            template
               module
                  helloworld.tpl
```

So now you know the basic directory structure of OpenCart module. The file structure is divided into two sections **admin** and **catalog**. The admin folders and files deal with the setting of the modules and data handling, while the catalog folders and files handle the frontend.

Let's start with an easy way to make a module. You are going to make the duplicate of the default Google Talk module of OpenCart and change it to the Hello World module. We are using Dreamweaver to work with files.

Changes made in the admin folder

Following are the steps to make changes in the admin folder:

1. Navigate to `admin/controller/module/` and copy `google_talk.php` and paste in the same folder. Rename it to `helloworld.php` and open it in your favorite text editor, then look for the following line of code:

   ```
   classControllerModuleGoogleTalk extends Controller {
   ```

   Change the class name to:

   ```
   classControllerModuleHelloworld extends Controller {
   ```

2. Now find `google_talk` and replace all with `helloworld` as shown in the following screenshot:

3. Then, save the file.

4. Navigate to `admin/language/english/module/` and copy `google_talk.php` and paste in the same folder; rename it to `helloworld.php` and open it. Then look for the following line of code:

   ```
   $_['entry_code'] = 'Google Talk Code:<br />
   <span class="help">Goto
     <a href="http://www.google.com/talk/service/badge/New"
       target="_blank">
       <u>Create a Google Talk chatback badge</u>
     </a> and copy &amp; paste the generated code into the
     text box.
   </span>';
   ```

5. And replace with following code:

```
$_['entry_code'] = 'Hello World Content';
```

6. Then again find `google_talk` and replace all with `helloworld`.

7. Then, save the file.

8. Navigate to `admin/view/template/module/` and copy the `google_talk.tpl` file and paste it in the same folder and rename it to `helloworld.tpl`; open it and look for `google_talk` and replace it with `helloworld` and save it.

Changes made in the catalog folder

Following are the steps to make changes in the catalog folder:

1. Go to `catalog/controller/module/` and copy the `google_talk.php` file and paste it in the same folder and rename it to `helloworld.php`; open it and look for the following line of code:

```
class ControllerModuleGoogleTalk extends Controller {
```

Change the class name to :

```
class ControllerModuleHelloworld extends Controller {
```

2. Now look for `google_talk` and replace all with `helloworld` and save it.

3. Navigate to `catalog/language/english/module/` and copy the `google_talk.php` file and paste it in the same folder and rename it to `helloworld.php`; open it and look for `Live Chat` and replace it with `Hello World` and save it.

4. Navigate to `catalog/view/theme/default/template/module/` and copy the `google_talk.tpl` file and paste it in the same folder and rename it to `helloworld.tpl`.

With the preceding file and code changes complete, our **Hello World** module is ready to be installed. Now log in to the admin section and navigate to **Extensions | Modules**, then look for **Hello World** and click on **[install]**, then click on **[Edit]** of the Hello World module. Then type the content that you would like to show on the frontend in the **Hello World Content** field. Now click on the **Add Module** button and adjust the settings as per your requirements and click on **Save**. With the settings as per the following image, the module will be shown in the User Account links box (**Login**, **My Account**, **Edit Account**, and so on) for the customer to access as per the layout and it will be shown in the right column, as the status is enabled. The following screenshot shows the settings for the **Hello World** module:

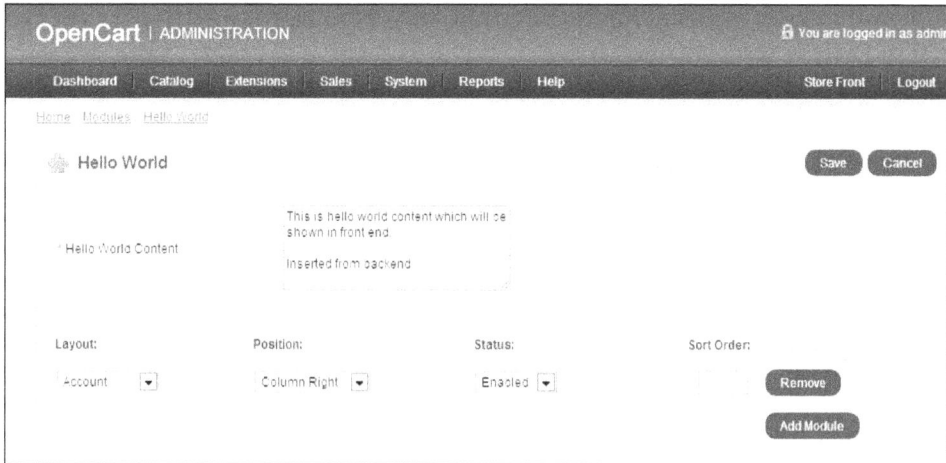

Now navigate to the frontend of the site and click on the **My Account** link on the home page; you will see the **Hello World** module as shown in the following screenshot:

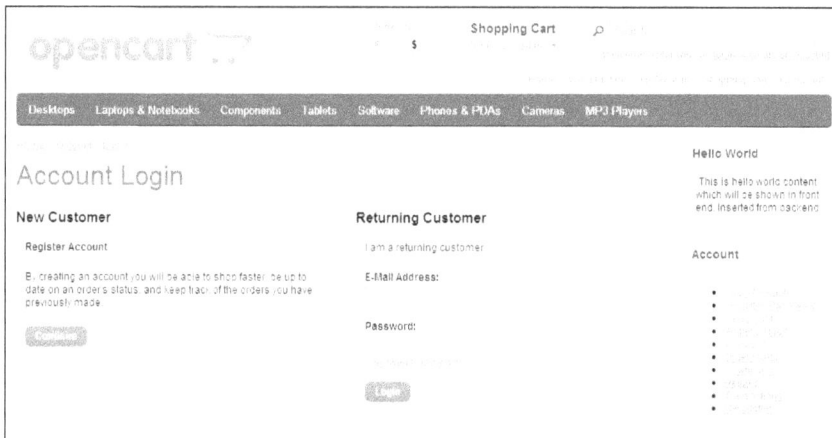

Following are the list of files that you need to upload to your live server:

- admin/language/english/module/helloworld.php
- admin/controller/module/helloworld.php
- admin/view/template/module/helloworld.tpl
- catalog/controller/module/helloworld.php
- catalog/language/english/module/helloworld.php
- catalog/view/theme/default/template/module/helloworld.tpl

By uploading the files, installing the module, and providing the settings, your Hello World module is ready to use.

You can change the Hello World text at `catalog/language/english/module/helloworld.php` to your desired text like `Welcome to our Store` and type the welcome message at the **Hello World Content** while setting the module and showing the welcome message at the frontend.

Installing, configuring, and uninstalling a module

There are many default modules in OpenCart. How modules get installed and which are the database tables that hold the settings of the module are really big questions for the developer.

Installing a module

Navigate to **admin | Extensions | Modules**, where you will find the list of modules. Click on **[Install]** and the module gets installed, as shown in the following screenshot:

🧩 Modules	
Module Name	Action
Account	[Edit] [Uninstall]
Category	[Edit] [Uninstall]
Google Talk	[Edit] [Uninstall]
Hello World	[Install]
Information	[Install]
Latest	[Edit] [Uninstall]

When you click on the **[Install]** module, the extension/module controller's install function is called. Now open `admin/controller/extension/module.php`, you will see the public function `install()`, which performs the permission check. If you get the Permission Denied! message, as shown in the following screenshot, you have to provide the access permission from **admin | User | User Group** and edit the user and check or tick mark the module/extension, so you will be able to edit the modules.

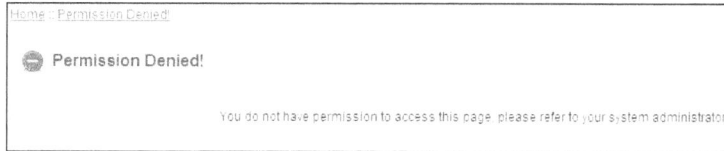

If you are provided the access, it loads the `admin/model/setting/extension.php` function `install()`.

```
public function install($type, $code) {
  $this->db->query("INSERT INTO " . DB_PREFIX ."extension SET `type`
= '" . $this->db->escape($type) . "', `code` = '" . $this->db-
>escape($code) . "'");
}
```

This means that data is inserted into the extension table of the database with type=module, and code=helloworld, in case of our Hello World module.

Configuring the module

After clicking on **[Install]** of the module, **[Edit] [Uninstall]** gets activated; after clicking on **[Edit]**, you will see the configuration section for the module. As per the Hello World module, the following screenshot shows the configuration section on clicking on **[Edit]**:

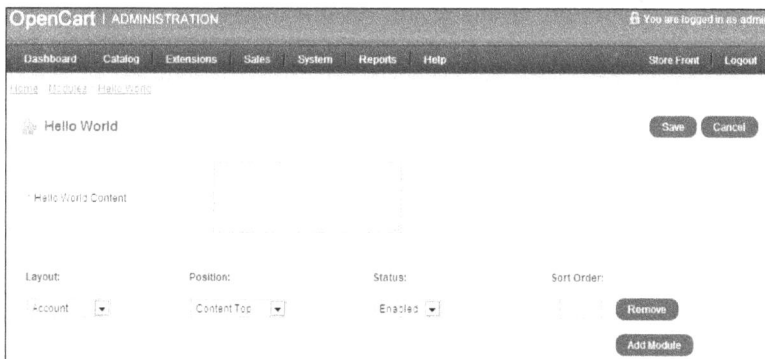

The **Hello World Content** field is saved in the `setting` table (`oc_setting` or as per the prefixes used during installation of OpenCart) of the database as per the name of the input box with group column of "helloworld". For this module, navigate to the file `admin/view/template/module/helloworld.tpl`, where you will find the following code:

```
<textarea name="helloworld_code" cols="40" rows="5"><?php echo
$helloworld_code; ?></textarea>
```

Thus, the message or text you typed in the text area is passed to the `admin/controller/module/helloworld.php` controller and the following lines of code is processed:

```
if (($this->request->server['REQUEST_METHOD'] == 'POST') && $this-
>validate()) {
  $this->model_setting_setting->editSetting('helloworld',
    $this->request->post);
  $this->session->data['success'] = $this->
    language->get('text_success');
  $this->redirect($this->url->link('extension/module',
    'token=' . $this->session->data['token'], 'SSL'));
}
```

It checks if the form is submitted through the POST method and checks whether the **Hello World Content** field is empty or not with the validate function. If the content is not empty and the form is submitted through the POST method, it calls the `editSetting` function which is in `admin/model/setting/setting.php`.

```
public function editSetting($group, $data, $store_id = 0) {
  $this->db->query("DELETE FROM " . DB_PREFIX . "setting WHERE
    store_id = '" . (int)$store_id . "' AND `group` = '" . $this-
      >db->escape($group) . "'");
  foreach ($data as $key => $value) {
    if (!is_array($value)) {
      $this->db->query("INSERT INTO " . DB_PREFIX . "setting SET
        store_id = '" . (int)$store_id . "', `group` = '" . $this-
          >db->escape($group) . "', `key` = '" . $this->db-
            >escape($key) . "', `value` = '" . $this->db-
              >escape($value) . "'");
    } else {
      $this->db->query("INSERT INTO " . DB_PREFIX . "setting SET
        store_id = '" . (int)$store_id . "', `group` = '" .
          $this->db->escape($group) . "', `key` = '" . $this->
            db->escape($key) . "', `value` = '" . $this->
              db->escape(serialize($value)) . "', serialized =
                '1'");
    }
  }
}
```

As given at the controller, `$group=helloworld`, `$data` is the `$_POST`, and `$store_id` is `0`. First it deletes all the Hello World settings and then starts to insert the new values. Following are the rows inserted in the `setting` table of the database:

setting_id	store_id	group	key	value	serialized
141	0	helloworld	helloworld_code	this is test	0
142	0	helloworld	helloworld_module	a:1 {i:0 a:4 {s:9 "layout_id" s:1 "6" s:8 "positio	1

If the value of the input field of the form is in array, the value is saved with `serialized`. Thus `serialized` becomes `1`, or else the value of `serialized` is `0`.

The `serialize($value)`, serialize function of PHP generates a storable representation of a value for an array.

`http://php.net/manual/en/function.serialize.php`

Layouts for the module

OpenCart has default page layouts that are based on the route of the page. Some of the layouts can be found at **admin | System | Design | Layouts**, and they are as follows:

- Account
- Affiliate
- Category
- Checkout
- Contact
- Default
- Home
- Information
- Manufacturer
- Product
- Sitemap

Now edit one of them, let's consider **Account**, as shown in the following screenshot:

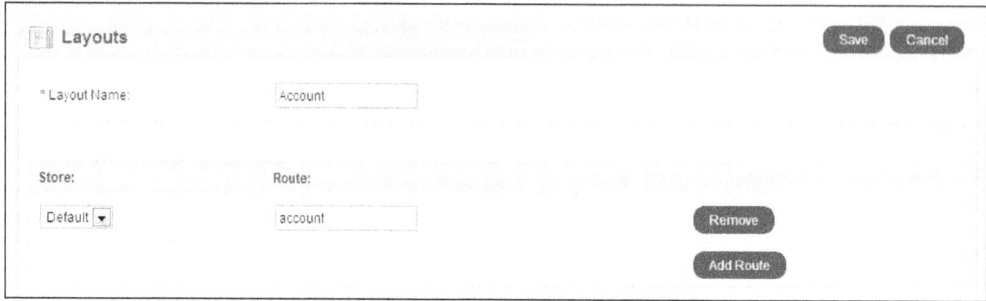

The value of **Route** is **account**; this means that the module will be seen where the route value contains account. If your URL is `http://example.com/index.php?route=account/login`, the module is shown as `route=account`. If you want to show the module in the account section, you have to change the layout to `Account`.

If you like to show the module in affiliate section, you have to choose the **Affiliate** layout as the route of **Affiliate**, that is, `route=affiliate` in the URL.

Similarly, for other layouts, check the route at **admin | System | Setting | Design | Layouts | Edit**, see the route, and check the URL route; you will find where the module will show on choosing the layout name.

Positions for the module

There are four positions for modules. They are as follows:

- Column Left
- Column Right
- Content Top
- Content Bottom

The following table shows the available positions for modules in the frontend.

Header		
Content Left	Content Top	Content Right
	Main Content	
	Content bottom	
Footer		

Choose as per your need of module position.

Status of the module

Status shows whether the module is enabled or disabled. If enabled, it is shown at the frontend, else it is not.

Sort order of the modules

If there is more than one module in any of the positions, sort order plays its role. Let us suppose two modules, **Hello World** and **Account**, are positioned to the right column of layout **Account**, and you like to show **Hello World** first, and then below it, the **Account** module, you have to insert **Sort order 1** for **Hello World** and **Sort order 2** for **Account**. If you do not insert sort order, it shows at the top. You will then be able to see the modules in the right column, as shown in the following screenshot:

Show same module in different layouts

We can easily show the same module in a different layout. To do this, click on the **Add Module** button and another row of the table is added; select the appropriate layout, position, status, and the sort order, then click on the **Save** button. You will be able to see the module in the respective layout. When you click on the **Add Module** button, the next row is added, as shown in the following screenshot:

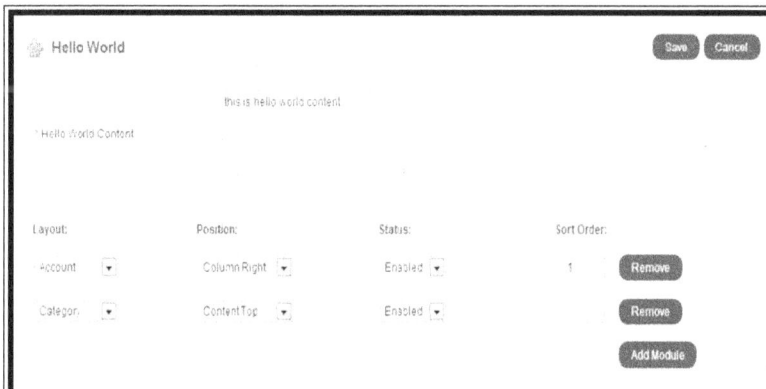

Effects of clicking on the Add Module button

The **Add Module** button shows another row for the module setting. Open `admin/catalog/view/template/helloworld.tpl` and you will see the following code, which is for the **Add Module** button:

```
<a onclick="addModule();" class="button"><?php echo
  $button_add_module; ?></a>
```

On clicking the **Add Module** link, the `addModule` function is called; the `addModule` function adds a row just below the previous row.

Uninstalling the module

Navigate to **admin | Extensions | Modules**, and you will find the list of modules. Just click on **[Uninstall]**, the module gets uninstalled and all settings get deleted. Let's see how it is done. Open `admin/controller/extension/module.php`, you will see the public function `uninstall()`,which performs the permission check and if there is permission access, it loads the model setting/extension uninstall function.

File structure – admin and frontend

When someone uses the module, it is reliable to have the admin section so that the user can handle the module functionality as well as position, layout, status, and sort order by which users can show the module wherever they like.

Creating the language files for the admin module in OpenCart

Language files are also named with `MODULENAME.php`. For example, let's say we want to create a file containing hello world messages or text; we have to create `helloworld.php`. Language files use "constant=value" configuration. The constant name is used in the code; it never changes, only the value for that language changes. If English language is active, it retrieves the constant from the English language folder's file; if another language is active, it retrieves from the other language folder's file. For example, if English language is active, the constant is taken from the English language folder's file.

```
$_['text_review'] = 'Product Review';
```

If Spanish language is active, the constant is taken from the Spanish language folder's file.

```
$_['text_review'] = 'De Revisión de Producto';
```

If German language is active, the constant is taken from the German language folder's file.

```
$_['text_review'] = 'ProduktBewertung';
```

A similar process is followed for the other languages installed.

Within the file, we will assign each line of text to a variable as $_['variablename']. The same variable name will be used in the controller to access the text or messages. For example, in the following code:

```
$this->data['heading_title'] = $this->language
    ->get('heading_title');
```

Now on, we will use the heading_title controller to access the "Hello World" text.

You can see the following code at admin/language/english/module/helloworld. php.

```
<?php
$_['heading_title']         = 'Hello World';
$_['text_module']           = 'Modules';
$_['text_success']          = 'Success: You have modified module
  Hello World!';
$_['text_content_top']      = 'Content Top';
$_['text_content_bottom']   = 'Content Bottom';
$_['text_column_left']      = 'Column Left';
$_['text_column_right']     = 'Column Right';
$_['entry_code']            = 'Hello World Content';
$_['entry_layout']          = 'Layout:';
$_['entry_position']        = 'Position:';
$_['entry_status']          = 'Status:';
$_['entry_sort_order']      = 'Sort Order:';
$_['error_permission']      = 'Warning: You do not have permission
  to modify module Hello World!';
$_['helloworld_content']         = Hello World Content';
?>
```

Creating the controller in the admin section of the OpenCart module

Controller is the core file where all the logic and magic take place. This is also where the variables for values and language are set and passed to the view variables for display. A Controller in OpenCart is simply a class file that is named in a way that can be associated with a URL.

Consider this URL: `http://example.com/index.php?route=module/helloworld`.

In the above example, OpenCart would attempt to find a controller file `helloworld.php` in the module folder with class `ControllerModuleHelloworld`.

We can see the code at `admin/controller/module/helloworld.php` whose functionalities are described as follows:

In OpenCart, controller class names must start with the controller and the folder on which the module is located and the filename without extension. For example, in the Hello World module, the class name for the controller is `ControllerModuleHelloworld` as it is inside the module folder and the filename is `helloworld.php`. Also, always make sure your controller extends the parent controller class.

```
class ControllerModuleHelloworld extends Controller {
```

Whenever the controller is called, the `index` function (public function `index()`) is always loaded by default.

```
$this->language->load('module/helloworld');
```

The preceding line of code loads the language file variables of `helloworld.php` which is in the module folder at `admin/language/*/module/helloworld.php` (* represents the language folder) and now you are able to get the text or messages with reference to variables like `$this->language->get('heading_title')`. This means the Hello World text is ready to transfer to the template files.

```
$this->document->setTitle($this->language->get('heading_title'));
```

The preceding line of code sets the title of the document Hello World.

The `$this->load->model('setting/setting')` variable loads the `setting.php` file of the setting folder which is in the model folder. As explained previously, it loads `admin/model/setting/setting.php`. Your module can load any model file in its controller file using the following code, if they are in the same `admin` or `catalog` folder as the controller. You will need to specify the path to the file you want to load from the `admin` folder within the parentheses. The preceding code will load the `settings` class so we have access to the functions within the `ModelSettingSetting` class in our model's controller file. Use the following format in your code to call a function from a loaded model file:

```
$this->model_setting_setting->editSetting('helloworld',
    $this->request->post);

if (($this->request->server['REQUEST_METHOD'] == 'POST') &&
    $this->validate()) {
```

```
$this->model_setting_setting->editSetting('helloworld',
  $this->request->post);
$this->session->data['success'] = $this->->
  language->get('text_success');
$this->redirect($this->url->link('extension/module',
  'token=' . $this->session->data['token'], 'SSL'));
  }
```

When a form is saved in the module section, the preceding lines of code, which are at `admin/controller/module/helloworld.php` run. If the code is submitted through the POST method and validates function return `true`, all the settings are saved to the database at the `setting` table and a success message is assigned to the success variable and is redirected to the list of the module page.

```
protected function validate() {
  if (!$this->user->hasPermission('modify', 'module/helloworld'))
  {
    $this->error['warning'] = $this->language
      ->get('error_permission');
  }
  if (!$this->request->post['helloworld_code']) {
    $this->error['code'] = $this->language->get('error_code');
  }
  if (!$this->error) {
    return true;
  } else {
    return false;
  }
}
```

When a form is submitted, validation is checked for whether permission is provided or not. It is checked whether the **Hello World Content** consists of the text or not. If no access is provided or no content is entered, error is returned true, by which it shows **Code Required** or **Permission Denied!** and alerts the user to provide the access or insert the content.

```
$this->data['heading_title'] = $this->language
  ->get('heading_title');
$this->data['text_enabled'] = $this->language
  ->get('text_enabled');
```

The `$this->language->get('heading_title')` variable gets the value of the `$_['heading_title']` variable from the language file `helloworld.php`, which is "Hello World" and is assigned to `$this->data['heading_title']`. Likewise, for `$this->language->get('text_enabled')`, "Enabled" is assigned to `$this->data['text_enabled']` and the same for the other files.

```
if (isset($this->error['warning'])) {
  $this->data['error_warning'] = $this->error['warning'];
} else {
  $this->data['error_warning'] = '';
}
```

The Hello World module checks for access permission and gives a warning if the user has no access to the module.

```
if (isset($this->error['code'])) {
  $this->data['error_code'] = $this->error['code'];
} else {
  $this->data['error_code'] = '';
}
```

If no content is inserted in the **Hello World Content** field and the user tries to save the module, it validates whether the content is inserted or not; if content is not inserted, an error is activated by which it will show the error code as "Code Required".

```
$this->data['breadcrumbs'] = array();
$this->data['breadcrumbs'][] = array(
  'text'      => $this->language->get('text_home'),
  'href'      => $this->url->link('common/home', 'token=' .
    $this->session->data['token'], 'SSL'),
  'separator' => false
);
$this->data['breadcrumbs'][] = array(
  'text'      => $this->language->get('text_module'),
  'href'      => $this->url->link('extension/module', 'token=' .
    $this->session->data['token'], 'SSL'),
  'separator' =>' :: '
);
$this->data['breadcrumbs'][] = array(
  'text'      => $this->language->get('heading_title'),
  'href'      => $this->url->link('module/helloworld', 'token=' .
    $this->session->data['token'], 'SSL'),
  'separator' =>' :: '
);
```

Breadcrumbs are defined in an array, and contain elements such as text, href, and separator. Text elements hold the word to show in the template file, href holds the link for the word, and separator holds what to use to separate between words. This is shown in the preceding lines of code.

```
'text'        => $this->language->get('text_home'),
```

The preceding line of code holds the "Home" word as per the language file.

```
'href'        => $this->url->link('common/home', 'token=' .
   $this->session->data['token'], 'SSL'),
```

The preceding line of code holds the link to the "Home" word.

```
'separator' => false
```

The preceding line of code holds the separator between the breadcrumbs; if no separator is needed, `false` is assigned.

```
$this->data['action'] = $this->url->link('module/helloworld',
   'token=' . $this->session->data['token'], 'SSL');
```

The preceding line of code will create a link and store it into the `action` variable. If we have to create the link in the admin area, we have to use it as explained previously. A token is used to preserve the admin user state.

```
$this->data['modules'] = array();
$this->data['modules'] = $this->config->get('helloworld_module');
```

An empty array is defined and we assign `$this->data['modules']` with all the settings of `helloworld_module`.

```
$this->load->model('design/layout');
```

It loads the `layout.php` file of the `design` folder which is in the `model` folder. As explained previously, it loads `admin/model/design/layout.php`. The preceding code will load the layout class, so we have access to the functions within the `ModelDesignLayout` class in our module's controller file.

```
$this->data['layouts'] = $this->model_design_layout->getLayouts();
```

The underscores (`model_design_layout`) refer to the file designations for `model/design/layout.php`. The `layouts` variable now holds all the layouts that are created at **System | Design | Layout** at the admin sections.

```
$this->template = 'module/helloworld.tpl';
$this->children = array('common/header','common/footer');
```

In the controller, you will need to load your module's template file in view. To do so, set $this->template to $this->template = 'module/helloworld.tpl', and it loads admin/view/template/module/helloworld.tpl.

```
$this->response->setOutput($this->render());
```

The $this->response->setOutput() variable sends data to the browser whether it's HTML or JSON and $this->render constructs the output HTML from the templates/data.

Creating the template file at admin in the OpenCart module

This refers to the template or TPL files. All variables that are passed from the controller to the view can be used for displaying the output of calculations or functionality.

Open the admin/view/template/module/helloworld.tpl file; we are describing the code taking some snippets only.

```
<?php echo $header; ?>
<?php echo $footer; ?>
```

The $header and $footer variables are passed from the controller as the template's children.

```
$this->children = array('common/header','common/footer');
```

With this, the content of the header and footer are shown on the module section.

Breadcrumbs section for the module

For keeping track of navigation, breadcrumbs are used; in the template file, breadcrumbs are shown by the following lines of code:

```
<div class="breadcrumb">
<?phpforeach ($breadcrumbs as $breadcrumb) {
  ?>
  <?php echo $breadcrumb['separator']; ?><a href="<?php echo
    $breadcrumb['href']; ?>"><?php echo $breadcrumb['text'];
  ?></a>
<?php } ?>
</div>
```

The `$breadcrumbs` array has been passed by the controller files. The `$breadcrumbs` array consists of the separator, URL link, and the text to show. All elements of the `$breadcrumbs` array are managed in the controller.

```php
<?php if ($error_warning) {
  ?>
  <div class="warning"><?php echo $error_warning; ?></div>
<?php } ?>
```

A warning will show up if you have no permission to access or edit the module. As for the Hello World module, it checks for permission and shows a warning if the user has no access to the module. The following screenshot shows the **Breadcrumbs**, **Header image and Title**, and **Header save and cancel button:**

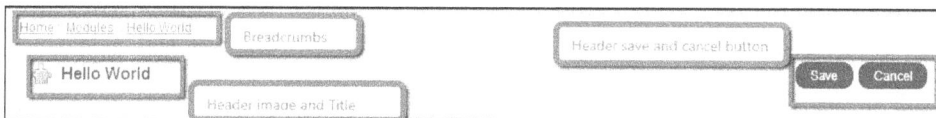

The following line of code shows the image icon near the heading title:

```php
<h1><imgsrc="view/image/module.png" alt="" /><?php echo
  $heading_title; ?></h1>
```

The following line of code shows the heading title that is passed from the controller:

```php
$this->data['heading_title'] = $this->language
  ->get('heading_title');
```

The following lines of code show the buttons to save and cancel:

```php
<div class="buttons">
  <a onclick="$('#form').submit();" class="button"><?php echo
    $button_save; ?></a>
  <a href="<?php echo $cancel; ?>" class="button"><?php echo
    $button_cancel; ?></a>
</div>
```

On clicking the **Save** button, the form with ID is submitted; on clicking the **Cancel** button, it calls the extension/module controller, which means it is redirected to the list of modules.

```php
<form action="<?php echo $action; ?>"
  method="post"enctype="multipart/form-data" id="form">
```

When the form code is initiated, it has `id=form`, which is used in the **Save** button to submit the form. When we click on the **Save** button, an action to the module / Hello World controller processes the submitted data.

The `<span class="required">*</span>` shows the asterisk (*) in red color by the style class required.

```
<textarea name="helloworld_code" cols="40" rows="5"><?php echo
  $helloworld_code; ?></textarea>
<?php if ($error_code) {
  ?>
  <span class="error"><?php echo $error_code; ?></span>
<?php } ?>
```

This is the text area field which holds some data; if this text area is submitted empty, it shows as an error.

```
<tr>
  <td class="left"><?php echo $entry_layout; ?></td>
  <td class="left"><?php echo $entry_position; ?></td>
  <td class="left"><?php echo $entry_status; ?></td>
  <td class="right"><?php echo $entry_sort_order; ?></td>
  <td></td>
</tr>
```

The table heading is shown by the preceding code and it will look as shown in the following screenshot:

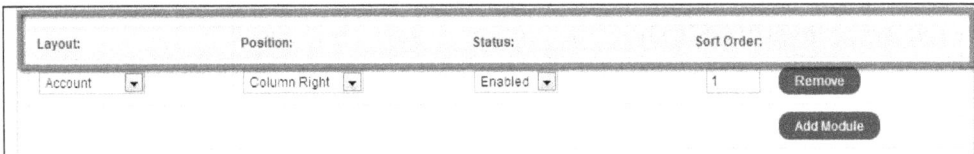

In the following code snippet, the `$module_row` variable is defined. It is assigned to zero and is increased with the `foreach` loop, so it is the count of the module rows that increases on clicking on the **Add Module** button.

```
<?php $module_row = 0; ?>
<?phpforeach ($modules as $module) { ?>
```

The `$modules` array carries the setting of the module; if it is empty, only the **Add Module** button is shown.

```
<select name="helloworld_module[<?php echo $module_row;
  ?>][layout_id]">
  <?php foreach ($layouts as $layout) {
  ?>
    <?php if ($layout['layout_id'] == $module['layout_id']) {
      ?>
      <option value="<?php echo $layout['layout_id']; ?>"
        selected="selected"><?php echo $layout['name'];
      ?></option>
    <?php } else { ?>
    <option value="<?php echo $layout['layout_id']; ?>"><?php echo
      $layout['name']; ?></option>
    <?php } ?>
  <?php } ?>
</select>
```

The preceding code shows the **Layout** option. If the layout id matches the module layout id, which has been already saved, the selected layout is shown among other layouts, else layouts are shown as default. The `layout` arrays have been passed from the controller. Similarly, for the position, select fieldname as `helloworld_module` with its second element as `position`.

```
<select name="helloworld_module[<?php echo $module_row;
  ?>][position]">
```

As we already know, there are four positions described in OpenCart; they are content top, content bottom, column left, and column right. The position module code for the content top is as follows:

```
<?php if ($module['position'] == 'content_top') {
  ?>
  <option value="content_top" selected="selected"><?php echo
    $text_content_top; ?></option>
<?php } else {
  ?>
  <option value="content_top"><?php echo $text_content_top;
  ?></option>
<?php } ?>
```

If module position is already defined and is equal to `content_top`, content top is selected, else others are selected as default. It works in a similar way for the content bottom, column left, and column right.

```
<select name="helloworld_module[<?php echo $module_row;
   ?>][status]">
 <?php if ($module['status']) {
    ?>
   <option value="1" selected="selected"><?php echo
     $text_enabled; ?></option>
   <option value="0"><?php echo $text_disabled; ?></option>
 <?php } else { ?>
   <option value="1"><?php echo $text_enabled; ?></option>
   <option value="0" selected="selected"><?php echo
     $text_disabled; ?></option>
 <?php } ?>
</select>
```

The preceding code is to show the module status; if module is `enabled`, `option value` is equal to `1`, else it is `0`. If module status is defined or equal to `1`, it shows that the module is already defined, so `enabled` is selected. If it is not defined, `disabled` is selected.

```
<input type="text" name="helloworld_module[<?php echo $module_row;
   ?>][sort_order]" value="<?php echo $module['sort_order']; ?>"
   size="3" />
```

The preceding code holds the sort order of the module.

```
<a onclick="$('#module-row<?php echo $module_row; ?>').remove();"
   class="button"><?php echo $button_remove; ?></a>
```

The preceding code line removes the rows when we click on the **Remove** button.

```
<a onclick="addModule();" class="button"><?php echo
   $button_add_module; ?></a>
```

On clicking on the **Add Module** link, function `addModule` is called, which adds a row just below the previous row.

```
function addModule() {}
```

The preceding function adds the rows for the modules setting. We can add as many modules as we like, just keep on clicking on the **Add Module** button. The following screenshot shows multiple rows for setting after clicking on the **Add Module** button:

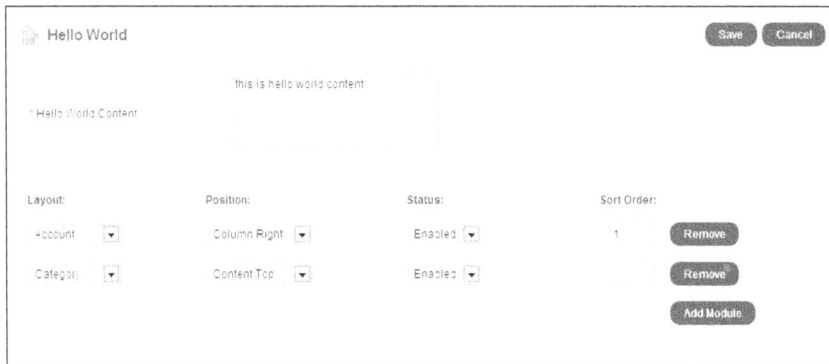

Creating the language file for catalog (frontend) module in OpenCart

You can create a language file in a similar way as we did in the admin section. For the frontend, your language file will be located at `catalog/language/english/module/MODULENAME.php`. The filename should be the same as the module name. As per the Hello World module, the language file name is `helloworld.php`, it is created at `catalog/language/english/module/` and consists only of the following code:

```php
<?php
  // Heading
  $_['heading_title']  = 'Hello World';
?>
```

The `Hello World` text is assigned to `heading_title`; with the same `heading_title`, it is accessible to the controller.

Creating the controller file for catalog (frontend) module in OpenCart

A controller file of a module for the frontend is found at `catalog/controller/module/MODULENAME.php`; as per the Hello World module, we can see the `helloworld.php` files at `catalog/controller/module`. Since we named the file `helloworld.php` and put it at `module/` folder, the controller classname will be `ControllerModuleHelloworld`.

```
class ControllerModuleHelloworld extends Controller {
```

Also, always make sure your controller extends the parent controller class so that it can inherit all its functions.

```
protected function index() {
```

The `index` function is always loaded by default if the second segment of the URL is empty. We can load the module controller at `http://example.com/index.php?route=module/helloworld/index` or `http://example.com/index.php?route=module/helloworld`.

Here the second segment of the URI is index; if you have created other functions, we can call the function of the module by passing it into the second segment of the URL.

```
$this->language->load('module/helloworld');
```

Loading of language files is done with the preceding line of code. According to the previous line, the `helloworld.php` file at `catalog/language/english/module/` is loaded if English language is active or it will load as per the language activated. For example, if Spanish language is active, it loads from `catalog/language/spanish/module/`.

```
$this->data['heading_title'] = $this->language->get('heading_title');
```

The preceding line fetches the text "Hello World" with `$this->language->get('heading_title');` and assigns it to the `heading_title` variable of the `data` array. The `$heading_title` file will show "Hello World" in the template files.

```
if (isset($this->request->server['HTTPS']) && (($this->request
  ->server['HTTPS'] == 'on') || ($this->request->server['HTTPS']
    == '1'))) {
    $this->data['code'] = str_replace('http', 'https',
      html_entity_decode($this->config->get('helloworld_code')));
    } else {
      $this->data['code'] = html_entity_decode($this->config
      ->get('helloworld_code'));
    }
```

The first line of code checks whether SSL is active. If SSL is active, the link's `http` of `$this->config->get('helloworld_code')` is replaced with `https`.

You will be able to get the value of the `setting` table in a database by passing the key. For example, consider the `setting` table of a database that consists of the following rows, as shown in the following screenshot:

setting_id	store_id	group	key	value	serialized
149	0	helloworld	helloworld_code	this is hello world content	0
150	0	helloworld	helloworld_module	a.1.{i.0.a.4.{s.9.''layout_id'' s.1.''6'' s.8 ''positio...	1
357	0	config	config_name	Dressing Shop	0
358	0	config	config_owner	Rupak	0
359	0	config	config_address	Kathmandu	0

If you want to show `Dressing Shop`, you can get it easily wherever you like in the controller, model, or template files. You just have to type the following line of code:

```
echo $this->config->get('config_name');
```

But if `serialized` is equal to `1`, it means that the value is stored in an array.

```
if (file_exists(DIR_TEMPLATE . $this->config
  ->get('config_template') . '/template/module/helloworld.tpl')) {
    $this->template = $this->config->get('config_template') .
      '/template/module/helloworld.tpl';
  } else {
    $this->template = 'default/template/module/helloworld.tpl';
  }
$this->render();
```

You can get an active template name from `$this->config->get('config_template');` the preceding lines of code check whether the `helloworld.tpl` file is on the active template or not. If the file is found in the active template, it uses it, or it will use one from the default template. It will be better if we keep the files on the default theme.

Creating the template file for catalog (frontend) module in OpenCart

You can find the template file at `catalog/view/theme/<template name>/module`; as for the Hello World module, the file name is `helloworld.tpl`. OpenCart frontend template files have deeper folder structures than the admin ones because admin sections can have only one template. For the frontend, on the other hand, there can be any number of templates; among them, one is selected from the **admin | system | setting | edit | the store** and at the **store** tab choose the best template under the **Template** field.

A folder named `<template name>` is created at `catalog/view/theme`. One of the basic rules in OpenCart is never to edit the default theme template file because if OpenCart does not find certain template files on your theme `<template name>` folder, it will find them on the default theme. While upgrading, the changes made on your custom theme will also get overridden. If template files are not found on the default theme, it shows the following error:

Notice: Error: Could not load template catalog/view/theme/customtheme/template/ module/helloworld.tpl! in system\engine\controller.php

Here, the theme folder's name is `customtheme`.

If you see this kind of error, it means that `helloworld.tpl` is missing on the `customtheme` and default theme folders. So you need to create the `helloworld. tpl` file at `catalog/view/theme/customtheme/template/module/` or `catalog/ view/theme/default/template/module/`. Since the `helloworld.tpl` file is not the default file of OpenCart, we can place it either on `customtheme` or in default theme.

If you require any changes on the default theme template files, you have to copy the files and folders to the `customtheme` folder and make changes on the `customtheme` folder's files, so upgrading it will help in preserving your changes. The following are the code on `catalog/view/theme/default/module/helloworld.tpl`.

```
<div class="box">
  <div class="box-heading"><?php echo $heading_title; ?></div>
  <div class="box-content" style="text-align: center;"><?php echo
    $code; ?></div>
</div>
```

The `$heading_title` file holds the text "Hello World" and `$code` holds the message or text that is inserted into the Hello World module at the backend.

Summary

In this chapter, we duplicated the Google_talk module to create the Hello World module. Hello World is created, installed, configured, and uninstalled. On configuration, we inserted some data and showed the same at the frontend.

We found out how code works in the Hello World module and its file and folder structure. We also described all the code that we used in the Hello World module's files. Taking reference of Hello World module, we should be able to go through other modules and become familiar with the modules of OpenCart.

2
Describing The Code of Extensions

In this chapter we will cover most of the code that is used in OpenCart to perform different functions, which will be helpful in creating modules. We have used OpenCart Version 1.5.5.1.

Global library methods

OpenCart has many predefined methods that can be called anywhere, such as in the `controller` folder or in the model, and in the view template files. You can find system level library files at `system/library/`. The following shows the different methods, how they can be written, and what their functions are:

- **Affiliate**: You can find most of the affiliate code under the affiliate section, and check the files at `catalog/controller/affiliate/` and likewise at `catalog/model/affiliate/`. The following are the list of methods we can use for the affiliate library:

  ○ `$this->affiliate->login($email, $password);`

  This command ensures that the e-mail and password are passed to the method. If the username (e-mail) and password match among the affiliates, it logs into the affiliate section. You can find this code at `catalog/controller/affiliate/login.php` on the validate function.

○ `$this->affiliate->logout();`

The affiliate is logged out. It means the affiliate ID will be cleared and its session will be destroyed, as well as the affiliate's first name, last name, e-mail, telephone number, and fax number are given empty values.

○ `$this->affiliate->isLogged();`

It checks whether the affiliate is logged in. If you want to show some message to the logged-in affiliate only, can you do so, as follows:

```
if($this->affiliate->isLogged()){
   echo "Welcome to the Affiliate Section";
}else {
   echo "You  are not at Affiliate Section";
}
```

○ `$this->affiliate->getId();`

When we echo the preceding line, it will show the active affiliate's ID.

○ `$this->affiliate->getFirstName();`

When we echo the preceding line, it will show the active affiliate's first name.

○ `$this->affiliate->getLastName();`

When we echo the preceding line, it will show the active affiliate's last name.

○ `$this->affiliate->getEmail();`

When we echo the preceding line, it will show the active affiliate's e-mail.

○ `$this->affiliate->getTelephone();`

When we echo the preceding line, it will show the active affiliate's telephone number.

○ `$this->affiliate->getFax();`

When we echo the preceding line, it will show the active affiliate's fax number.

○ `$this->affiliate->getCode();`

When we echo the preceding line, it will show the active affiliate's tracking code, which is used to track referrals.

- **Cache**: It consists of the cache files and is located under `system/cache`.

  - `$this->cache->get($key);`

    You can retrieve the cache file as per the `key` value passed with this method.

    In the following example, if the cache file of `country` is found in the `system/cache` folder, it directly takes the data from there , else performs database queries to retrieve the country:

    ```
    $country_data = $this->cache->get('country');
    if (!$country_data) {
      $query = $this->db->query(
        "SELECT * FROM " . DB_PREFIX ."country
          ORDER BY name ASC");
      $country_data = $query->rows;
      $this->cache->set('country', $country_data);
    }
    return $country_data;
    ```

  - `$this->cache->set($key, $value);`

    It helps in creating the cache files. Considering the preceding example about the `country` cache file, if the cache file is not found in the `system/cache` folder, then queries to the database are performed and the retrieved data is set with the key of the country.

  - `$this->cache->delete($key);`

    It deletes the file in the `cache` folder as per the `key` value provided.

    For example: `$this->cache->delete('country');` deletes the country cache file.

- **Captcha**: Captcha functions are not automatically instantiated; you have to access them as follows:

  - Write the `captcha` function under `controller` as follows:
    ```
    public function captcha() {
      $this->load->library('captcha');
      $captcha = new Captcha();
      $this->session->data['captcha'] = $captcha->getCode();
      $captcha->showImage();
    }
    ```

- ○ When the template file is called, the Captcha image is shown.

  ```
  <img src="index.php?route=controller/captcha" alt="" />
  ```

  "controller/captcha" in the preceding code line is the path where you make the captcha function. For example, if you write the function in the information/information.php file, it will be information/ information.

- **Cart**: System-instantiated cart objects are available for use. They are as follows:

  - ○ `$this->cart->getProducts();`

    It gives the list of all products in the array of the cart.

  - ○ `$this->cart->add($product_id, $qty = 1, $option = array());`

    It adds products to the cart; just pass the product ID, your desired quantity, and your desired options.

  - ○ `$this->cart->update($key, $qty);`

    If you need to update a product in the cart, this method is used where $key is the product ID and $qty is the quantity you added.

  - ○ `$this->cart->remove($key);`

    If you want to remove a product from the cart, this method is used where $key is the product ID that you wish to remove.

  - ○ `$this->cart->clear();`

    If you wish to remove all the products at once, this method is used.

  - ○ `$this->cart->getWeight();`

    It gives the sum of the weight of all products in the cart which requires shipping.

  - ○ `$this->cart->getSubTotal();`

    It gives the subtotal of all products which are in the cart before being taxed.

  - ○ `$this->cart->getTaxes();`

    It gives the array of total taxes applied to the cart.

  - ○ `$this->cart->getTotal();`

    It gives the total of all products in the cart after being taxed.

- ○ `$this->cart->countProducts();`

  It gives the total number of products in the cart.

- ○ `$this->cart->hasProduct();`

  It checks whether the cart has products or not.

- ○ `$this->cart->hasStock();`

  It checks for the stock of each product in the cart. If it has stock, it returns `true`; else `false` (means no stock).

- ○ `$this->cart->hasShipping();`

  It checks whether each product in the cart has shipping or not. If a product has shipping, `true` is returned; else `false`.

- ○ `$this->cart->hasDownload();`

  It checks whether each product in the cart is downloadable or not. If a product is downloadable, `true` is returned; else `false`.

- **Config**: The `config` values are loaded from the `Settings` table of the database.

  - ○ `$this->config->set($key, $value);`

    It is used to override the `$key` value of the "`Settings`" table value of the database. It does not save the value to the database.

    For example, if you want to show a different store name than the set value in the database, we add the following code in the `controller` folder:

    ```
    $this->config->set('config_name','New Store Name');
    ```

    Normally, when we echo `$this->config->get('config_name');` we get the store name; however since the set value is changed now, we will get the store name as "`New Store Name`".

  - ○ `$this->config->get($key);`

    It returns the set value as per the `$key` value passed. If there is no key value, it returns `null`. For example, when you echo `$this->config->get('config_name');`, you will get the store name.

- **Currency**: It consists of the methods that can be applied to currencies:

    ◦ `$this->currency->set($currency);`

    It sets or overrides the `currency` code to be used in the session as well as sets the cookie for the currency.

    ◦ `$this->currency->format($number, $currency='', $value='', $format=true)`

    It formats the number to the currency passed. For example, if you have the number `100` and currency `USD`, it will be formatted to `$100.00`. Here `$number` is the price value, `$currency` is the currency code, `$value` is the conversion rate between the currencies, and `$format` is to format the currencies. For example

    `$this->currency->format(50, 'USD', 1, false);`

    gives **50.00** as the output and

    `$this->currency->format(50, USD, 1, true);`

    gives **$50.00** as the output.

    By navigating to **Admin | System | Localization | Currencies**, we can find the settings where we insert the currency, the currency sign, the position of the sign, the decimal points to show, and so on.

    ◦ `$this->currency->convert($value, $from, $to);`

    If currency is set from **Admin | System | Localization | Currencies**, the value passed is converted from a certain chosen currency to another.

    ◦ `$this->currency->getId($currency='');`

    If you need the ID of the currency, we have to use the `getId()` method. For example, by using `$this->currency->getId('USD');`, you will get the ID of the US dollar. `USD` is the code for the currency inserted.

    If no currency code is defined, it returns `zero`.

    ◦ `$this->currency->getSymbolLeft(($currency='');`

    Some currencies' symbols appear to the left of the value; for example, $100 in the case of 100 US dollars. We can get the symbol on the left side of the value with the use of the method. Now, echo `$this->currency->getSymbolLeft('USD');`

- ○ `$this->currency->getSymbolRight(($currency='');`

  Some currencies' symbols appear on the right side of the value, for example, the Swedish, 100krona. We can get the symbol on the right side of the value with this method. Now, echo `$this->currency->getSymbolRight('SEK');`

- ○ `$this->currency->getDecimalPlace($currency='');`

  Navigate to **Admin | System | Localization | Currencies | Insert Button**, where there is a **Decimal Places** field to insert the currency. The setting is activated as per the activated currency. If we insert 2 in the input field and then save it after the decimal, two values are displayed: **$100.00**. Now, echo `$this->currency->getDecimalPlace('USD');`

- ○ `$this->currency->getCode();`

  It returns you the ISO code that you inserted at **Admin | System | Localization | Currencies | Insert Button**.

- ○ `$this->currency->getValue($currency = '');`

  It gives the set value of the **Value** field while inserting the currency. It is taken as the exchange rate for the specified currency with respect to the default currency.

- ○ `$this->currency->has($currency);`

  It checks whether the passed currency exists in the OpenCart currency list. If it finds the currency, it returns `true`; else `false`.

- **Customer**: It consists of the customer data.

  - ○ `$this->customer->login($email, $password, $override = false);`

    It logs a customer in. It checks for the customer's username and password when `$override` is passed `false`, else only for current logged in status and the e-mail. If it finds the correct entry, the OpenCart wish list entries are retrieved. In addition to this, customer ID, first name, last name, e-mail, telephone, fax, newsletter subscription status, customer group ID, and address ID can also be globally accessed by the customer. It also updates the customer IP address from where he/she logs in.

- ○ `$this->customer->logout();`

  When it is called, it logs out the customer. First of all, it updates the OpenCart wish list field of the customer table in the database and destroys the customer's session ID. Then, it assigns a blank value to the customer object's data such as customer ID, first name, last name, e-mail, telephone, fax, newsletter, customer group ID, and address ID.

- ○ `$this->customer->isLogged();`

  It checks whether the customer is logged in or not. If he/she is logged in, it returns `true` else `false`. For instance, consider the following lines of code:

  ```
  if($this->customer->isLogged()){
     echo "You are at the logged customer section";
  }else{
     echo "You have not logged in yet";
  }
  ```

- ○ `$this->customer->getId();`

  When you echo it, it gives you the customer ID of the logged-in customer.

- ○ `$this->customer->getFirstName();`

  When we echo this line, we will show the active customer's first name.

- ○ `$this->customer->getLastName();`

  When we echo the preceding line, it will show the active customer's last name.

- ○ `$this->customer->getEmail();`

  When we echo the preceding line, it will show the active customer's e-mail address.

- ○ `$this->customer->getTelephone();`

  When we echo the preceding line, it will show the active customer's telephone number.

- ○ `$this->customer->getFax();`

  When we echo the preceding line, it will show the active customer's fax number.

- $this->customer->getFirstName();

  When we echo the preceding line, it will show the active customer's first name.

- $this->customer->getNewsletter();

  When we echo the preceding line, it will show either 0 or 1, if 1 is shown, it means the customer is subscribed to the newsletter. If zero is shown, it means the customer is not subscribed to the newsletter.

- $this->customer->getCustomerGroupId();

  When we echo the preceding line, it will show the active customer's group ID.

- $this->customer->getBalance();

  When we echo the preceding line, it will show the active customer's current balance. When you view the "Your Transaction" link after logging in to the customer section, you will find the total current balance; the same balance is shown by this code.

- $this->customer->getRewardPoints();

  When we echo the preceding line, it will show the active customer's total remaining reward points earned.

- **Database**: The db class helps to query the database to perform insert, select, delete, and update, as well as providing methods to clean the data by escaping, getting the last inserted ID, and the total count of rows.

  - $this->db->query($sql);

    It executes the passedsql statement. For instance, consider the following lines of code:

    ```
    $query = $this->db->query("SHOW COLUMNS FROM
      `".DB_PREFIX."product` LIKE 'youtube'");
    if(!$query->num_rows){
      $this->db->query("ALTER TABLE `".DB_PREFIX."product`
                        ADD `youtube` TEXT NOT NULL");
    }
    ```

    These lines of code are written in the controller file or model files of OpenCart. The method searches for the YouTube column in the product table, and if it is not found, it alters the product table by adding another column named YouTube.

- $this->db->escape($value);

    It escapes or cleans the data before entering it to the database to avoid the SQL injection. Developers perform this for security reasons.

- $this->db->countAffected($sql);

    It returns the count of affected rows from the most recent query execution.

- $this->db->getLastId($sql);

    It returns the ID of the last inserted row from the most recent query execution.

- **Document**: Document library methods can be called from `controller`, only before rendering the document.

    - $this->document->setTitle($title);

        This line of code sets the page's title.

    - $this->document->getTitle();

        This line of code gets the page's title.

    - $this->document->setDescription($description);

        This line of code gets the page's meta description.

    - $this->document->getDescription();

        This line of code gets the page's meta description.

    - $this->document->setKeywords($keywords);

        This line of code sets the page's keyword meta tag.

    - $this->document->getKeywords();

        This line of code gets the page's keyword meta tag.

        For the home page of OpenCart, the title and description keywords are accessed from the settings inserted at **System | Settings | Edit** and under the **Store** tab. And for other pages, title and description is set as defined to override the default values as per the need in the `controller` file.

○
```
$this->document->addLink($href, $rel);
```

It adds the link at the head section as follows:

```
$this->document->addLink($this->url->link(
  'product/product', 'product_id=42','canonical');
```

If we write the preceding line of code in the `controller` file, we will see the following code at the head sections:

```
<link href="http://example.com/index.php?route=
  product/product&product_id=42"rel="canonical" />
```

A canonical page is the preferred version of a set of pages with highly similar content.

> Why specify a canonical page? It's common for a site to have several pages listing the same set of products. For example, one page might display the products sorted in alphabetical order, while other pages display the same products listed by price or by rating.
>
> Details of a canonical page can be found at the following URL:
>
> ```
> http://support.google.com/webmasters/bin/answer.
> py?hl=en&answer=139394
> ```

○
```
$this->document->getLinks();
```

It lists the set links. Mostly, calls are made in the header of `controller`.

○
```
$this->document->addStyle($href, $rel = 'stylesheet',
$media = 'screen');
```

It adds the extra style sheet needed only in the page. For example, consider the following lines of code:

```
$this->document->addStyle('catalog/view/javascript/
  jquery/colorbox/colorbox.css');
```

The `colorbox.css` file is needed in the `product` details page, so it is called in `catalog/controller/product/product.php` and the style sheet is added to the `<head>` section of the document.

○ `$this->document->getStyles();`

It lists the style sheet at the `<head>` section of the document. Mostly, calls are made in the header `controller`.

As with the `addStyle` method, `colorbox.css` is added, so a line is added in the `<head>` section of the document. The following is the line we can see on the `<head>` section of the document.

```
<link rel="stylesheet"type="text/css"href=
  "catalog/view/javascript/jquery/colorbox/colorbox.css
    "media="screen" />
```

○ `$this->document->addScript($script);`

It adds the script files (for example, JavaScript files) needed only in the page. For example:

```
$this->document->addScript('catalog/view/javascript/
  jquery/tabs.js');
```

This adds the `tabs.js` files wherever the preceding line of code is added.

○ `$this->document->getScripts();`

It lists the script files added with the `addScript` method. Just as the `addScript` code in the preceding example, where the `tabs.js` file is added, the following line of code is added in the `<head>` section of the document:

```
<script type="text/javascript"src="catalog/view/
  javascript/jquery/tabs.js"></script>
```

- **Encryption**: You can find the `encryption` file at `system/library/encryption.php` which has the `Encryption` class and its object name is `encryption`. It is used to encrypt and decrypt the values.

  ○ `$this->encryption->encrypt($value);`

  It encrypts the data based on the key in the `admin` settings.

  ○ `$this->encryption->decrypt($value);`

  It decrypts the data based on the key in the `admin` settings.

- **Language**: You can find all the data under `catalog/language`:
    - ○ `$this->language->get($key);`

        It gets the value of the key from the `language` file. For example:

        `$this->language->get('heading_title');`

        It searches for the value of `heading_title` in the `language` file.

    - ○ `$this->language->load($filename);`

        It loads the `language` file and makes its variable for use.

        `$this->language->load('catalog/category');`

        It loads the `catalog/language/english/catalog/category.php` file when the English language is active or loads the respective language's `category.php`.

- **Length**: You can find the `length` file at `system/library/length.php` which has the `Length` class and its object name is `length`. It is used to convert, format, and get the unit of length.
    - ○ `$this->length->convert($value, $from, $to);`

        The passed value is converted as per the value provided. For example, consider the following lines of code:

        ```
        $length = $this->length->convert($this->config->get(
          'ups_length'), $this->config->get(
            'config_length_class_id'), $this->config->get(
              'ups_length_class_id'));
        ```

        The configured length is converted to the UPS length.

    - ○ `$this->length->format($value, $length_class_id, $decimal_point = '.', $thousand_point = ',');`

        The passed value is formatted to the required length format.

    - ○ `$this->length->getUnit($length_class_id);`

        It returns the length's unit, such as cm or inches.

- **Log**: You can find all the log files stored under `system/logs`.

  ○ `$this->log->write($message);`

  It writes the message passed on to the `system/logs/error.txt` file. For example:

  ```
  $this->log->write('This is the error message');
  ```

  If you write this code and then refresh the URL which calls this file, the **This is the error message** message is logged in the `error.txt` file.

- **Mail**: You are shown an example directly for `mail`, which will help you understand the concept more clearly. With the following lines of code, an e-mail is sent:

  ```
  $mail = new Mail();
  $mail->setTo($this->request->post['email']);
  $mail->setFrom($this->config->get('config_email'));
  $mail->setSender($this->config->get('config_name'));
  $mail->setSubject(html_entity_decode($subject, ENT_QUOTES,
    'UTF-8'));
  $mail->setText(html_entity_decode($message, ENT_QUOTES,
    'UTF-8'));
  $mail->send();
  ```

  The `setTo()` method sets the receiver to whom the mail is addressed, the `setFrom()` method sets the sender's e-mail ID , `setSender()` sets the name of the sender, `setSubject()` sets the subject section of the mail, `setText()` sets the text for the message if it's only text (if it is an HTML e-mail, we use `setHtml()`), and the `send()` method sends the mail.

- **Pagination**: The following code snippet is a part of the user listing.

  ```
  $pagination = new Pagination();
  $pagination->total = $user_total;
  $pagination->page = $page;
  $pagination->limit = $this->config->get(
    'config_admin_limit');
  $pagination->text = $this->language->get(
    'text_pagination');
  $pagination->url = $this->url->link('user/user', 'token=
    ' . $this->session->data['token'] . $url .'&page={page}',
      'SSL');
  $this->data['pagination'] = $pagination->render();
  ```

`total` is the total number of users, `page` is the page number that is available through the `GET` value, `limit` is defined by the setting in the admin, `text` shows the numbers and extra messages, and `url` is to move to other pages. With this rendering `$pagination` is available for the template view to show the page numbers.

- **Request**: Two commonly used methods for a request-response communication between a client and server are `GET` and `POST`. In OpenCart, these are written as follows:

  ○ `$this->request->get;`

  ○ `$this->request->post;`

For a selected element, it is respectively written as:

  ○ `$this->request->get['selected'];`

  ○ `$this->request->post['selected'];`

- **Response**: You can find the response system files at `system/library/response.php`, which have a class name of `Response` and its object name is `response`.

  `$response = new Response();`

  ○ `$response->addHeader('Content-Type: text/html; charset=utf-8');`

    The `addheader()` method adds the content type used by the document.

  ○ `$this->redirect($url);`

    It redirects the page to the URL specified. `$url` passed should have the complete URL.

- **Session**: It stores the active session data:

  ○ `$this->session->getId()`

    It returns the active session ID.

- **Tax**: System-initiated tax objects are used in OpenCart. They are as follows:

  ○ `$this->tax->setShippingAddress($country_id, $zone_id);`

    It sets the shipping address with the country ID and zone ID.

- ○ `$this->tax->setPaymentAddress($country_id, $zone_id);`

  It sets the payment address with the country ID and zone ID.

- ○ `$this->tax->setStoreAddress($country_id, $zone_id);`

  It sets the store address with the country ID and zone ID.

- ○ `$this->tax->calculate($value, $tax_class_id, $calculate = true);`

  It calculates the tax, only if `$tax_class_id` is set and `$calculate` is set to `true`.

- **URL**: It helps in making the full URL. You can find the URL file at `system/library/url.php` which has the class name `url` and its object name is `url`.

  - ○ `$this->url->link($route, $args = '', $connection = 'NONSSL')`

    It makes the URL to be passed as the `$route` variable. If SSL is active, it makes `https://`; else `http://`.

- **User**: You can find most of the user code under the `account` section, and you can check the files at `catalog/controller/account/`. The following are the list of methods we can use for the user library:

  - ○ `$this->user->getId();`

    When we echo the preceding line, it will show the active user's ID.

  - ○ `$this->user->login($username, $password);`

    When the username and password are passed to the method, and if they match among the users, it logs in to the administration section.

  - ○ `$this->users->logout();`

    The admin user gets logged out. It means that the user ID will be cleared, its session will be destroyed, and the user's username and user ID are assigned empty values.

  - ○ `$this->users->isLogged();`

    It checks if the user is logged in or not.

○   `$this->users->hasPermission($key, $value);`

It checks whether the user has permission or not. For example:

```
if (!$this->user->hasPermission('modify',
  'catalog/category')) {
$this->error['warning'] = $this->language->get(
'error_permission');
}
```

The preceding code checks whether the user is provided access to modify or insert the categories. Permission for users can be provided by navigating to **Admin | System | Users | User Group**, where one can edit or insert a new user and provide the necessary permission to the user.

○   `$this->users->getId();`

It returns the active user's ID.

○   `$this->users->getUserName();`

It returns the active user's username.

- **Weight**: You can find the `weight` file at `system/library/weight.php` which has a class name `Weight` and its object name is `weight` and is used to convert, format, and get the unit of weight.

  ○   `$this->weight->convert($value, $from, $to);`

  The passed value is converted as per the value provided to the desired weight. The `$value` attribute is the weight of the products on the shopping cart, `$from` is the weight class needed to be converted, and `$to` is the required weight class. You can insert and edit the weight class by navigating to **Admin | System | Weight Class**.

  ○   `$this->weight->format($value, $weight_class_id,`
        `$decimal_point = '.', $thousand_point = ',');`

  The passed value is formatted to the required weight format.

  ○   `$this->length->getUnit($weight_class_id);`

  It returns the weight's unit, such as kg, pound, or gram.

Detailed description of the Featured module

The Featured module highlights specific products so that they will be helpful in increasing the sales and lets users know which products are highlighted.

Configuring the Featured module in OpenCart 1.5.5.1

In this section, you will see how to configure the Featured module in OpenCart and likewise you can configure other modules as per the requirements:

1. Log in to the **Administrator** dashboard, hover over the **Extensions** tab, and then click on **Modules** to see a list of modules. If the **Featured** module is not already installed, click on **[Install]**.

2. In order to configure a featured product, click on **[Edit]**. On clicking, the following screen is seen:

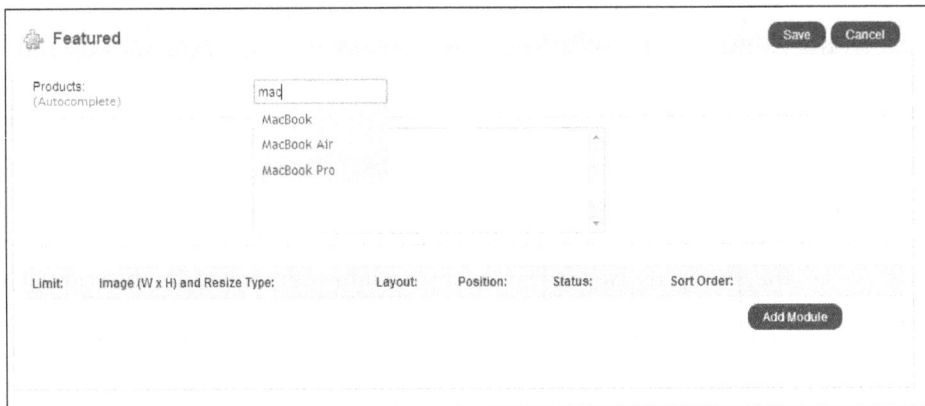

3. Now start typing the name of the products, and it will auto complete and pop-out the list of the name of the products that matches the words with the product name. Choose the product that you want to show at the featured products, and it will show in the list.

4. Now, to add another product, just type again and choose the right product. By doing this, make the list of featured products. If you do not want the products on the featured list, just click on the red minus sign to the right of the product and the product will be removed from the list.

5. Now click on the **Add Module** button and provide the setting for the appearance of the module. Some setting columns are:

   ° **Limit**: This indicates the number of products to show. Although we insert many products, only a limited number of products are shown.

   ° **Image (W x H) and Resize Type**: This option is used to insert the width and height of the image to be shown for the respective layout and position.

   ° **Layout**: This is the page where the featured products will be shown.

   ° **Position**: This option indicates the place where the module will be shown.

   ° **Status**: This option is shown at the frontend only if it is enabled.

   ° **Sort Order**: This option indicates the order in which it will be displayed at the frontend.

6. Add as many modules as you wish in different layouts and positions and then click on **Save**.

Exploring the code used in the Featured module

When you click on **[Edit]** of the installed `Featured` module, the route `module/featured` is called. It means that there are files named `featured.php` in the `module` folder in `controller`. So let's start with listing the files used by the `Featured` module:

- `admin/controller/module/featured.php`
- `admin/language/english/module/featured.php`
- `admin/view/template/module/featured.tpl`
- `catalog/controller/module/featured.php`
- `catalog/language/english/module/featured.php`
- `catalog/view/theme/default/template/module/featured.tpl`

Exploring the featured.php file under the admin folder

OpenCart's `Controller` is simply a class file that is named in a way that can be associated with a URI. The class name should start with the word `Controller` followed by the folder name and the file name. For example:

```
class ControllerModuleFeatured extends Controller {
```

The preceding code line creates the `Controller` class of the `Featured` module. The class name starts with `Controller`, followed by the module folder, and then the featured file. The `Featured` module's `Controller` file is named as `featured.php` and is in the module folder. As always, it has extended the `Controller` parent.

If the file name consists of an underscore (_), there will be no problems with respect to the class name. Everything except the underscore needs to be the same. If your `Controller` file is named with an underscore, you have to make the `language` file with an underscore as well. Never use an underscore for the class name.

Most of the related code is already described in *Chapter 1, Getting Started with OpenCart Modules*, so you have the description of the code and how it works functionally. By default, the `index()` method is called unless the second segment is passed in the URI. While clicking on **[Edit]**, no second segment is passed, so it runs the `index()` method, which loads the `language` files named `featured.php` in the module folder in the language section, and sets the title of the document as follows:

```
$this->document->setTitle($this->language->get('heading_title'));
```

It then loads the model file, `setting.php`, and when the module is saved, it validates the data by checking the permission and checking whether the image size is inserted or not. Check the `validate()` method, find out how it returns `true` when validation is successful and assigns the error message; it returns `false` if there is some error, such as permission denied and/or the image's height and width are not entered.

```
if (isset($this->request->post['featured_module'])) {
  foreach ($this->request->post['featured_module'] as
    $key => $value) {
    if (!$value['image_width'] || !$value['image_height']) {
      $this->error['image'][$key] = $this->language->get(
        'error_image');
    }
  }
}
```

The preceding code shows how the error message gets activated if height and/or width are not inserted on saving the module.

```
$this->data['heading_title'] = $this->language->get(
    'heading_title');
$this->data['text_enabled'] = $this->language->get(
    'text_enabled');
$this->data['text_disabled'] = $this->language->get(
    'text_disabled');
```

The text and messages to be shown at view are assigned from the `language` files to data variables; you can see similar lines of code which perform this function:

```
if (isset($this->error['image'])) {
    $this->data['error_image'] = $this->error['image'];
} else {
    $this->data['error_image'] = array();
}
```

If someone forgets to insert the height and/or width of the image, the error messages to be shown are assigned. The breadcrumbs are defined in an array as follows:

```
$this->data['breadcrumbs']
```

And the `action` links are defined as follows:

```
$this->data['action'] = $this->url->link('module/featured',
    'token=' . $this->session->data['token'], 'SSL');
```

The list of products that you have inserted is submitted in `$_POST['featured_product']` and all the product IDs are separated by a comma. Similarly, the products stored in the database for the `Featured` module are also saved with their product IDs separated by commas:

setting_id	store_id	group	key	value	serialized
39	0	featured	featured_product	43,40,42,49,46,47,28	0
40	0	featured	featured_module	a:1:{i:0;a:8:{s:5:"limit";s:1:"6";s:11:"image_widt...	1

The following code checks whether the product is submitted and then takes the product IDs from the POST method; if not, it takes from the database value:

```
if (isset($this->request->post['featured_product'])) {
    $products = explode(',', $this->request->post[
        'featured_product']);
} else {
    $products = explode(',', $this->config->get(
        'featured_product'));
}
```

`$products` is run through a loop to make an array of products' names and IDs and is passed to the template view.

```
$this->data['modules'] = $this->config->get('featured_module');
```

The preceding line of code retrieves the settings of the Featured module from the database. Other parts of the code are similar to those defined in the Hello World module, in *Chapter 1, Getting Started with OpenCart Modules*, and the same logics are applied to the language file, so we don't need to describe these here.

Exploring the featured.tpl file under admin folder

We will be describing only the extra code snippets, as most of them are already described in the Hello World module.

The most distinguishing section in the Featured module is the autocomplete input box. For that, let's create an input box as follows:

```
<input type="text" name="product" value="" />
```

Whenever a user starts to type in the text box, the following code starts to work:

```
$('input[name=\'product\']').autocomplete({
```

It searches for similar-named products as follows:

```
admin/index.php?route=catalog/product/autocomplete
```

If it finds products, the product, on clicking, gets appended to the featured product ID's `<div>` element and a product list is generated. The code is shown in the `admin/view/template/module/featured.tpl` file as follows:

```
$('#featured-product').append('<div id="featured-product' +
  ui.item.value + '">' + ui.item.label + '<imgsrc=
    "view/image/delete.png" alt="" /><input type="hidden" value=
      "' + ui.item.value + '"/></div>')
```

When the red minus sign, to the right of the product, is clicked, the following code snippet gets activated that deletes the rows of product:

```
$('#featured-product div img').live('click', function() {
  $(this).parent().remove();
  $('#featured-product div:odd').attr('class', 'odd');
  $('#featured-product div:even').attr('class', 'even');
  data = $.map($('#featured-product input'), function(element){
    return $(element).attr('value');
  });
```

```
$('input[name=\'featured_product\']').attr('value',
   data.join());
});
```

Exploring the featured.php file under the catalog folder

Only the extra code snippets are described, as most of them are discussed in *Chapter 1, Getting Started with OpenCart Modules,* and most of them are similar to the `Hello World` module.

```
$products = explode(',', $this->config->get('featured_product'));
```

If we echo `$this->config->get('featured_product')`, we will get the product IDs that are separated by commas. Thus, the `$products` array is assigned by separating the product IDs by commas.

```
if (empty($setting['limit'])) {
   $setting['limit'] = 5;
}
```

If there is no limit inserted while setting the `Featured` module, it will show only five products.

```
$products = array_slice($products, 0, (int)$setting['limit']);
```

An iteration is performed using `foreach` to the `$products` array, and with the help of `$this->model_catalog_product->getProduct($product_id);`, all details of the product are retrieved and only the required elements are assigned to the `$products` array to be passed to the template file as follows:

```
$this->data['products'][] = array(
   'product_id' => $product_info['product_id'],
   'thumb' => $image,
   'name' => $product_info['name'],
   'price' => $price,
   'special' => $special,
   'rating' => $rating,
   'reviews' =>sprintf($this->language->get('text_reviews'),
      (int)$product_info['reviews']),
   'href' => $this->url->link('product/product',
      'product_id=' . $product_info['product_id'])
);
```

With the preceding code, only the required data such as `product_id`, `thumb`, and `name` are assigned to the array that will be shown in the template file.

The code of `catalog/view/theme/default/template/module/featured.tpl` are similar to the `Hello World` module template file. Here, products that are added on the backend are shown. The `$products` array is received from the `controller` file, which consists of the product ID, thumb of image, name, price, special price, rating, reviews, and link to the product details. The same data are shown in the `Featured` module's frontend.

The Shipping module

OpenCart has many prebuilt shipping modules. Navigate to **Admin | Extensions | Shipping**, it lists out the `Shipping` module as shown in the following screenshot:

Shipping Method	Status	Sort Order	Action
Australia Post	Disabled		[Edit] [Uninstall]
Citylink	Disabled		[Install]
Fedex	Disabled		[Install]
Flat Rate	Disabled	1	[Edit] [Uninstall]
Free Shipping	Disabled		[Edit] [Uninstall]
Per Item	Disabled		[Install]
Parcelforce 48	Disabled		[Install]
Pickup From Store	Disabled		[Install]
Royal Mail	Disabled		[Install]
total cost Based Shipping	Enabled		[Edit] [Uninstall]

You have to install and configure it, and it will be shown at the frontend under **Shipping Methods** while performing a checkout.

As you already know, modules or extensions can be created by cloning an existing one that functions in a similar way to what you want. So, for `Shipping`, we will be cloning any one of them that fulfills our requirement. For example, if you want the shipping cost to be charged as per the total cost purchased, you can clone the weight-based shipping module; likewise, if you want to make DHL shipping rates module using the live rate, look up from the DHL site. You need to start with the existing **UPS** shipping extension.

Let's start to make the `Shipping` module that is based on the total cost purchased.

Changes made in the admin folder

In this section we will see the changes that are to be made in the `admin` folder to create the shipping module:

1. Navigate to `admin/controller/shipping/` and copy `weight.php` and paste it in the same folder. Rename it to `totalcost.php`, open it in your favorite text editor, and then find the following lines:

   ```
   class ControllerShippingWeight extends Controller {
   ```

   Change the class name as follows:

   ```
   class ControllerShippingTotalcost extends Controller {
   ```

   Now find "`weight`" and replace all with "`totalcost`". Then, save the file.

2. Navigate to `admin/language/english/shipping` and copy `weight.php` and paste in the same folder and rename it to `totalcost.php` and open it. Then find "`Weight`" and replace all with "`Total Cost`".

   After performing the replace, find the following code:

   ```
   $_['entry_rate']  = 'Rates:<br /><span class=
     "help">Example: 5:10.00,7:12.00 Total Cost:
       Cost, totalcost:Cost, etc..</span>';
   ```

   Then perform the following changes:

   ```
   $_['entry_rate']  = 'Total cost:Rates:<br />
     <span class="help">Example: 100:10.00,200:20.00
       Total Cost:ShippingCost, TotalCost:Shipping Cost,
         etc.</span>';
   ```

3. Navigate to `admin/view/template/shipping`, copy the `weight.tpl` file, and paste it in the same folder. Rename it to `totalcost.tpl`, open it, then find "`weight`", replace it with "`totalcost`", and then save it.

Changes made in the catalog folder

After the changes are made in the `admin` folder, we will now see the changes to be made in the `catalog` folder to create the shipping module.

1. Go to `catalog/model/shipping`, copy the `weight.php`, paste it in the same folder, and rename it to `totalcost.php`. Open it and find the following line:

   ```
   class ModelShippingWeight extends Model {
   ```

Change the class name as follows:

```
class ModelShippingTotalcost extends Model {
```

Now find "weight" and replace all with "totalcost". After performing the replacement, find the following lines of code:

```
$totalcost = $this->cart->gettotalcost();
```

And perform the following changes:

```
$totalcost = $this->cart->getSubTotal();
```

Our requirement is to show the shipping cost as per the total cost purchased, so we have performed this change.

Now, find the following lines:

```
if ((string)$cost != '') {
$quote_data['totalcost_' . $result['geo_zone_id']] =
  array('code'=>'totalcost.totalcost_' . $result[
    'geo_zone_id'],'title' => $result['name'] . '
      (' . $this->language->get('text_totalcost') . '
        ' . $this->totalcost->format($totalcost, $this->
          config->get('config_totalcost_class_id')) . ')',
'cost'=> $cost,
'tax_class_id' => $this->config->get(
  'totalcost_tax_class_id'),
'text'=> $this->currency->format($this->tax->calculate(
  $cost, $this->config->get('totalcost_tax_class_id'),
    $this->config->get('config_tax'))));
}
```

As we need only the name, change the following line of code:

```
'title'=> $result['name'] . ' (' . $this->language->get(
  'text_totalcost') . '' . $this->totalcost->format(
    $totalcost, $this->config->get(
      'config_totalcost_class_id')) . ')',
```

To the following:

```
'title' => $result['name'],
```

Weight has different classes such as kilogram, gram, and pound, but in our total cost purchased, we did not have any class specified, so we have removed it.

Now click on **Save**.

2. Go to `catalog/language/english/shipping` and copy the `weight.php` file and paste it in the same folder and rename it to `totalcost.php`. Open it and find "Weight" and replace it with "Total Cost"

With these changes, the module is ready to be installed. Navigate to **Admin | Extensions | Shipping**, find **Total Cost Based Shipping**, click on **[Install]**, provide the permission to modify and access to the user, and then edit to configure it. In the general tab, make a change in the **Status** field to **Enabled**. Other tabs are loaded as per the **Geo Zone** setting. For default, **UK Shipping** and **UK VAT Zone** are set as **Geo Zone**:

3. Now insert **Total cost Rates**. If the subtotal reaches `100` and the shipping cost is `20`, we have to insert `100:20`.

4. If the customer tries to order more than the inserted total cost, shipping is deactivated.

5. In this way, you can now clone the `Shipping` modules and make the changes on the logics as necessary.

The Payment module

Any module can be made by cloning an existing module with similar functionality as it will make coding very easy and fast. You can view the list of `Payment` modules by navigating to **Admin | Extensions | Payments**.

Now you can also make the `Payment` module similar to the `Shipping` module. While making the `Payment` module, we have to work out in the `Payment` folder.

Before starting to write a payment module, you need to know the on-site payment and off-site payment, which are the broad categories of the payment methods.

Off-site payment

Off-site payment means making payment to the payment service by redirecting to the payment service website and making the transaction; upon success or failure, they are returned back to the relevant pages. If payment is successful, it shows the success page, else it will show the failure message.

Some of the off-site payment modules are: PayPal Standard, Moneybookers, LiqPay, PayPoint, and so on.

If you are using the off-site payment, choose one of the off-side payment modules of OpenCart and then clone your desired `Payment` modules.

On-site payment

Payments are made on the same site with on-site payment; it means the customer never leaves your site to make the payment. Some of the on-site OpenCart payment modules are: Authorize.net AIM, PayPal Pro, SagePay Direct, and so on.

If using on-site payment, it is suggested to have the SSL certificate and SSL enabled on the setting in OpenCart.

If you are using on-site payment, choose one of the on-site payment modules and clone it and make your desired module.

Most of the code will be the same, only the `controller` file, `catalog` and some time view template forms need to be changed while creating the `Payment` modules.

The Order Total module

Order totals are those modules which affect the total price of the order. You can find the list of order totals at **Admin | Extensions | Order Totals**. Some of them are:

*   **Coupon**: This option allows the customer to apply the coupon discount
*   **Store Credit**: If you have store credit, it automatically decreases the total purchase cost with the available credit

Sub-Total:	$702.00
UK Shipping:	$35.00
Eco Tax (-2.00):	$6.00
VAT (17.5%):	$122.85
Store Credit:	$-865.85
Total:	$0.00

- **Handling Fee**: This option provides an additional fee for handling the product
- **Low Order Fee**: This option provides extra cost if the customer orders the minimum specified quantity
- **Reward Points**: Points are accumulated which can be used to buy reward points products
- **Sub-Total**: This option shows the subtotal separately
- **Taxes**: This option shows taxes separately
- **Total**: This option shows the total amount to be billed
- **Gift Voucher**: This option is used to gift credit to purchase the products

When they are applied, there is a change in the **Total** value, so they are placed on the `Order Totals` module. You will be able to see the `Order totals` module in the next chapter. We will show you how to create the `Order totals` modules. We will go in depth with the `Tips Order Total` module, as when someone likes to add `Tips`, there is an increase on the order total.

Summary

In this chapter, we explored most of the system level libraries that OpenCart provides. We explored most of the extra code used in the `Featured Product` module by which you are now able to know the code flow of the OpenCart module. Likewise, we created a new `Shipping` module, which shows the shipping cost according to the total cost purchased by cloning the weight-based shipping. Similarly, we discussed the payment module of OpenCart and the ways to clone it. With this, you are able to start coding with OpenCart **Extensions** (**Modules**, **Payments**, and **Shipping**).

3
Creating Custom OpenCart Modules

In this chapter we will create a Feedback module and a Tips module and show how code works and are managed. You already know how to duplicate or clone the module, as explained in *Chapter 1, Getting Started with OpenCart Modules*, and likewise know most of the global methods, which make it easy for you to create a module. In the Feedback module, visitors will be able to write feedback about the site, and the feedback provided will be approved by the admin and shown at the frontend. At last, we will create the Order Total module as tips get added to the order total.

Getting started with feedback management

We will show you the way to create the **admin** form and the **list** page, after this we will move forward to make the frontend pages where visitors can submit their feedback and lists of the feedback. As always, we will start with analyzing our requirements and seeing which part of OpenCart resembles them, so that we can clone the pages, making it easy to work with the code.

Database tables for feedback

We start by making tables at the database. As OpenCart is multistore, multilanguage support and can be shown at many layouts, we need to take care of those as well. For these, we have to make approximately four tables: `feedback`, `feedback_description`, `feedback_to_layout`, and `feedback_to_store`.

In the following screenshot, `oc_` is the database prefix we use while installing Opencart. If you are not sure about the database prefix, you can see the `config.php` file at the root folder of the OpenCart, open it, and find the line "`define('DB_PREFIX'`". You will see `define('DB_PREFIX', 'oc_');` and as per this the database prefix is `oc_`. The `oc_feedback` table stores the status, sort order, date added, and date modified with the feedback ID. The `oc_feedback_description` table stores the author name, feedback given, and language ID for multiple languages. The `oc_feedback_to_store` table saves the store ID and feedback for the particular store of OpenCart whose feedback needs to be shown as OpenCart are multistores, and the `oc_feedback_to_layout` table stores to whichever layout the feedback module is to be shown.

The following screenshot shows the database schema:

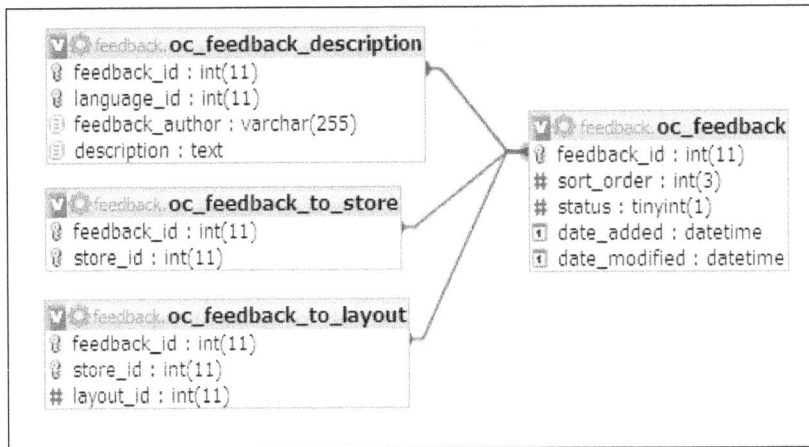

The following are the queries that need to run in the database to create the feedback table, feedback description table, feedback to layout table, and feedback to store table. If you have used a prefix other than the `oc_`, change `oc_` to that prefix on the following query; only then it will be ready to run.

```
CREATE TABLE IF NOT EXISTS `oc_feedback` (
  `feedback_id` int(11) NOT NULL AUTO_INCREMENT,
  `sort_order` int(3) NOT NULL DEFAULT '0',
  `status` tinyint(1) NOT NULL,
  `date_added` datetime NOT NULL DEFAULT '0000-00-00 00:00:00',
  `date_modified` datetime NOT NULL DEFAULT '0000-00-00 00:00:00',
  PRIMARY KEY (`feedback_id`)
) ENGINE=MyISAM  DEFAULT CHARSET=utf8 AUTO_INCREMENT=5 ;
```

```
CREATE TABLE IF NOT EXISTS `oc_feedback_description` (
  `feedback_id` int(11) NOT NULL,
  `language_id` int(11) NOT NULL,
  `feedback_author` varchar(255) NOT NULL,
  `description` text NOT NULL,
  PRIMARY KEY (`feedback_id`,`language_id`)
) ENGINE=MyISAM DEFAULT CHARSET=utf8;

CREATE TABLE IF NOT EXISTS `oc_feedback_to_layout` (
  `feedback_id` int(11) NOT NULL,
  `store_id` int(11) NOT NULL,
  `layout_id` int(11) NOT NULL,
  PRIMARY KEY (`feedback_id`,`store_id`)
) ENGINE=MyISAM DEFAULT CHARSET=utf8;

CREATE TABLE IF NOT EXISTS `oc_feedback_to_store` (
  `feedback_id` int(11) NOT NULL,
  `store_id` int(11) NOT NULL,
  PRIMARY KEY (`feedback_id`,`store_id`)
) ENGINE=MyISAM DEFAULT CHARSET=utf8;
```

After running the preceding query on database, we now will start to make the custom page to list out all the feedback with pagination and a form to edit and insert the feedback at the admin section. Then, we will move to the frontend pages. As you know, OpenCart follows the MVC framework, so you need to manage the files likewise. For the feedback, you need to create files as shown in the following screenshot:

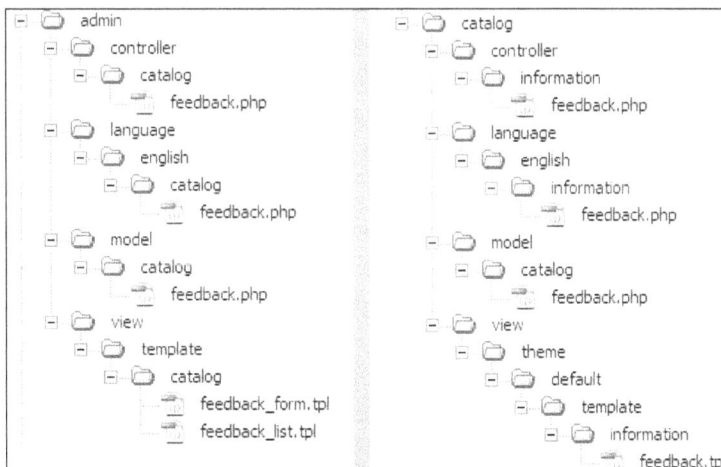

Creating files at the admin section for feedback

At the admin section, we will create files that will create a list of feedback and also a form to insert or edit the feedback and save it into the database. For this, we will start with the language file, which is the easiest one.

Creating the language file at the admin section

Create a file at `admin/language/english/catalog/feedback.php`, and paste the following lines of code:

```php
<?php
$_['heading_feedback']= 'Feedback';

$_['heading_feedback_author']= 'Feedback';
$_['text_success']        = 'Success: You have modified feedback!';
$_['text_default']        = 'Default';
$_['column_feedback_author']= 'Feedback Author';
$_['column_sort_order'] = 'Sort Order';
$_['column_action']       = 'Action';
$_['entry_feedback_author']= 'Feedback Author:';
$_['entry_description'] = 'Feedback Description:';
$_['entry_store']         = 'Stores:';
$_['entry_status']        = 'Status:';
$_['entry_sort_order']  = 'Sort Order:';
$_['entry_layout']        = 'Layout Override:';
$_['error_warning']       = 'Warning: Please check the form
  carefully for errors!';
$_['error_permission']  = 'Warning: You do not have permission to
  modify feedback!';
$_['error_description'] = 'Description must be more than 3
  characters!';
$_['error_store']         = 'Warning: This feedback page cannot be
  deleted as its currently used by %s stores!';
?>
```

The preceding lines of code are written to describe the text that is set to variable for the language, which can be accessed and used in the controller files.

Creating the model file at the admin section

To create a model file, you need to make a model folder, and in this folder, it will be called at the controller as `$this->load->model(FOLDER_NAME/FILE_NAME_WITHOUT_EXTENSION')`. For the feedback, you have to create a file named `feedback.php` at `admin/model/catalog/feedback.php`. Thus, you can load this file at controller as `this->load->model('catalog/feedback')`.

After creating the file, you need to make a unique class name starting with the word `Model`, followed by the folder name, and then file name without extensions. So, for our feedback, the class name will be `ModelCatalogFeedback`, which extends the parent `Model` class.

```php
<?php
class ModelCatalogFeedback extends Model {
  public function addfeedback($data) {
    $this->db->query("INSERT INTO " . DB_PREFIX . "feedback SET
      sort_order = '" . (int)$data['sort_order'] . "', status = '"
      . (int)$data['status'] . "'");
    $feedback_id = $this->db->getLastId();
    foreach ($data['feedback_description'] as $language_id =>
    $value) {
      $this->db->query("INSERT INTO " . DB_PREFIX .
        "feedback_description SET feedback_id = '" .
        (int)$feedback_id . "', language_id = '" .
        (int)$language_id . "',  feedback_author= '" . $this->db
        ->escape($value['feedback_author']) . "', description = '"
        . $this->db->escape($value['description']) . "'");
    }
    if (isset($data['feedback_store'])) {
      foreach ($data['feedback_store'] as $store_id) {
        $this->db->query("INSERT INTO " . DB_PREFIX .
        "feedback_to_store SET feedback_id = '" .
        (int)$feedback_id . "', store_id = '" . (int)$store_id .
        "'");
      }
    }
    if (isset($data['feedback_layout'])) {
      foreach ($data['feedback_layout'] as $store_id => $layout) {
        if ($layout) {
          $this->db->query("INSERT INTO " . DB_PREFIX .
            "feedback_to_layout SET feedback_id = '" .
            (int)$feedback_id . "', store_id = '" . (int)$store_id
            . "', layout_id = '" . (int)$layout['layout_id'] .
            "'");
```

```
                }
              }
            }
          $this->cache->delete('feedback');
        }
      }
```

The preceding code shows how we can query the database. We have to start with `$this->db->query()` and inside the braces we write the SQL query that we have already seen in the global methods in *Chapter 2, Describing The Code of Extensions*. As per the preceding code, `$this->db->query()` inserts the feedback ID, sort order, and status on the `feedback` table and retrieves the feedback ID that was inserted last and assigns it to `$feedback_id`. Also, `$data['feedback_description']` is looped as you can have multiple descriptions because it can contain many languages. Thus, it inserts the feedback ID, language ID, author, and feedback description into the description table. As OpenCart supports the multistore and multiple layouts, you must take care of them. After the insertion of the description, we have to run the store query to insert the store followed by the layout insertion. Then a cache is deleted if it was already created.

```php
public function editfeedback($feedback_id, $data) {
    $this->db->query("UPDATE " . DB_PREFIX . "feedback SET
      sort_order = '" . (int)$data['sort_order'] . "', status = '" .
      (int)$data['status'] . "' WHERE feedback_id = '" .
      (int)$feedback_id . "'");
    $this->db->query("DELETE FROM " . DB_PREFIX .
      "feedback_description WHERE feedback_id = '" .
      (int)$feedback_id . "'");
    foreach($data['feedback_description'] as $language_id => $value)
    {
      $this->db->query("INSERT INTO " . DB_PREFIX .
        "feedback_description SET feedback_id = '" .
        (int)$feedback_id . "', language_id = '" . (int)$language_id
        . "', feedback_author= '" . $this->db
        ->escape($value['feedback_author']) . "', description = '" .
        $this->db->escape($value['description']) . "'");
    }
    $this->db->query("DELETE FROM " . DB_PREFIX . "feedback_to_store
      WHERE feedback_id = '" . (int)$feedback_id . "'");
    if (isset($data['feedback_store'])) {
      foreach ($data['feedback_store'] as $store_id) {
        $this->db->query("INSERT INTO " . DB_PREFIX .
          "feedback_to_store SET feedback_id = '" .
          (int)$feedback_id . "', store_id = '" . (int)$store_id .
          "'");
```

```
      }
    }
    $this->db->query("DELETE FROM " . DB_PREFIX .
      "feedback_to_layout WHERE feedback_id = '" . (int)$feedback_id
      . "'");
    if (isset($data['feedback_layout'])) {
      foreach ($data['feedback_layout'] as $store_id => $layout) {
        if ($layout['layout_id']) {
          $this->db->query("INSERT INTO " . DB_PREFIX .
          "feedback_to_layout SET feedback_id = '" .
          (int)$feedback_id . "', store_id = '" . (int)$store_id .
          "', layout_id = '" . (int)$layout['layout_id'] . "'");
        }
      }
    }
    $this->db->query("DELETE FROM " . DB_PREFIX . "url_alias WHERE
      query = 'feedback_id=" . (int)$feedback_id. "'");
    $this->cache->delete('feedback');
  }
```

The queries update the database table row of feedback, feedback description, feedback store, and feedback layout. The first query shown in the code will update the feedback table row, but for other tables of feedback description, feedback store, and feedback layout, it first deletes all the related feedback as per the feedback ID and then inserts them again. When the feedback table is updated, it deletes all the related feedback description in the feedback_description table and then inserts the updated data; although no changes are made, it takes them as the new value and inserts this in the loop. The same is done for feedback_to_layout and feedback_to_store. Then it deletes the cache if it is already created.

```
  public function deletefeedback($feedback_id) {
    $this->db->query("DELETE FROM " . DB_PREFIX . "feedback WHERE
      feedback_id = '" . (int)$feedback_id . "'");
    $this->db->query("DELETE FROM " . DB_PREFIX .
      "feedback_description WHERE feedback_id = '" .
      (int)$feedback_id . "'");
    $this->db->query("DELETE FROM " . DB_PREFIX . "feedback_to_store
      WHERE feedback_id = '" . (int)$feedback_id . "'");
    $this->db->query("DELETE FROM " . DB_PREFIX .
      "feedback_to_layout WHERE feedback_id = '" . (int)$feedback_id
      . "'");
    $this->cache->delete('feedback');
  }
```

The preceding code is used to delete the feedback; you have to take care to delete data from all the tables whenever you use the delete operation. As per our feedback, you have to delete data from the `feedback`, `feedback_description`, `feedback_to_store`, and `feedback_to_layout` tables as well as the cache file.

```
public function getfeedback($feedback_id) {
  $query = $this->db->query("SELECT * FROM " . DB_PREFIX .
    "feedback WHERE feedback_id = '" . (int)$feedback_id . "'");
  return $query->row;
}
```

The preceding code snippet is used to retrieve a row; to run a select query, you have to run the query with `$this->db->query()`, and then assign to some variable and run with `$Variable_Name->row;`. To retrieve a single column and to retrieve multiple rows, we have to write `$Variable_Name->rows;`, which returns an array. As per our SQL query, we just need a single row of the specified feedback ID so we have performed `$query->row;`.

```
public function getfeedbackDescriptions($feedback_id) {
  $feedback_description_data = array();
  $query = $this->db->query("SELECT * FROM ".DB_PREFIX .
    "feedback_description WHERE feedback_id ='". (int)$feedback_id
    ."'");
  foreach ($query->rows as $result) {
    $feedback_description_data[$result['language_id']] = array(
    'feedback_author' => $result['feedback_author'],
    'description' => $result['description']);
  }return $feedback_description_data;
}
```

The preceding code retrieves the description of the respective feedback ID passed and will return all the languages' description as well as return the description in an array.

```
public function getTotalFeedbacks() {
  $query =$this->db->query("SELECT COUNT(*) AS total FROM
    ".DB_PREFIX."feedback");
  return $query->row['total'];
}
```

The preceding lines of code return the total number of feedback.

```
public function getfeedbacks($data = array()) {
  if ($data) {
```

```
        $sql = "SELECT * FROM " . DB_PREFIX . "feedback f LEFT JOIN "
          . DB_PREFIX . "feedback_description fd ON (f.feedback_id =
          fd.feedback_id) WHERE fd.language_id = '" . (int)$this
          ->config->get('config_language_id') . "'";
        $sort_data = array('fd.feedback_author','f.sort_order');
        if (isset($data['sort']) &&in_array($data['sort'],
          $sort_data)) {
            $sql .= " ORDER BY " . $data['sort'];
            } else {$sql .= " ORDER BY fd.feedback_author";
      }
      if (isset($data['order']) && ($data['order'] == 'DESC')) {
        $sql .= " DESC";
      } else {$sql .= " ASC";
    }
  if (isset($data['start']) || isset($data['limit'])) {
    if ($data['start'] < 0) {  $data['start'] = 0; }
    if ($data['limit'] < 1) {  $data['limit'] = 20; }
    $sql .= " LIMIT " . (int)$data['start'] . "," .
      (int)$data['limit'];
  }
$query = $this->db->query($sql);
return $query->rows;
} else {
  $feedback_data = $this->cache->get('feedback.' . (int)$this-
    >config->get('config_language_id'));
  if (!$feedback_data) {
    $query = $this->db->query("SELECT * FROM " . DB_PREFIX .
      "feedback f LEFT JOIN " . DB_PREFIX . "feedback_description
      fd ON (f.feedback_id = fd.feedback_id) WHERE fd.language_id
      = '" . (int)$this->config->get('config_language_id') . "'
      ORDER BY fd.feedback_id.");
    $feedback_data = $query->rows;
    $this->cache->set('feedback.' . (int)$this->config
      ->get('config_language_id'), $feedback_data);
  }
  return $feedback_data;
  }
}
```

For retrieving all the feedback from the database we use the preceding code. The `$data` array, which is passed in the function, holds the sort order, order by, limit of rows, and helps in filtering, sorting, and limiting the rows from the whole data. If `$data` is set, it retrieves data from the SQL query and retrieves the required rows by filtering as per `$data`; else it tries to retrieve from the cache files if it is already set. If it does not find the cache, it again runs the query and retrieves the rows of feedback and sets the cache and returns the array of feedback. It will retrieve the data from the `feedback` and `feedback_description` table and return as an array. It is sorted by passed data as name or so on, else by default, it is sorted by `$feedback_id`.

```
public function getfeedbackStores($feedback_id) {
  $feedback_store_data = array();
  $query = $this->db->query("SELECT * FROM " . DB_PREFIX .
    "feedback_to_store WHERE feedback_id = '" . (int)$feedback_id
    . "'");
  foreach ($query->rows as $result) {
    $feedback_store_data[] = $result['store_id'];
  }
  return $feedback_store_data;
}
```

The preceding code returns all stores that the specified feedback ID passed.

```
public function getfeedbackLayouts($feedback_id) {
  $feedback_layout_data = array();
  $query = $this->db->query("SELECT * FROM " . DB_PREFIX .
    "feedback_to_layout WHERE feedback_id = '" . (int)$feedback_id
    . "'");
  foreach ($query->rows as $result) {
    $feedback_layout_data[$result['store_id']] =
      $result['layout_id'];
  }
  return $feedback_layout_data;
}
```

The preceding code returns all the layouts of the specified feedback ID passed.

```
public function getTotalfeedbacksByLayoutId($layout_id) {
  $query = $this->db->query("SELECT COUNT(*) AS total FROM " .
    DB_PREFIX . "feedback_to_layout WHERE layout_id = '" .
    (int)$layout_id . "'");
  return $query->row['total'];
}
?>
```

The `getTotalfeedbacksByLayout` function will return the number of feedback counts that the `layout_id` has passed and closes the main model class. In this way, you can create the model file and make any kinds of data retrieval, insertion, and deletion work and these will be used on the controller files by loading the model file.

Creating the controller file at the admin section

Now you will see the `controller` file of admin that controls all the code insert, list, delete, and form sections. You will get a description on each of them. Create a file at `admin/controller/catalog/feedback.php` and start to insert the following lines of code:

```php
<?php
class ControllerCatalogFeedback extends Controller {
  private $error = array();
  public function index() {
    $this->language->load('catalog/feedback');
    $this->document->setTitle($this->language
      ->get('heading_feedback'));
    $this->load->model('catalog/feedback');
    $this->getList();
  }
}
```

You created a controller named `ControllerCatalogFeedback`, which is extended from the parent called `Controller`. Next, you made the `index` function, which gets loaded by default. Within that, it loads the language files you have already created, and the title is set with the feedback heading and loaded with the `feedback.php` model file.

```php
public function insert() {
  $this->language->load('catalog/feedback');
  $this->document->setTitle($this->language
    ->get('heading_feedback'));
  $this->load->model('catalog/feedback');
  if (($this->request->server['REQUEST_METHOD'] == 'POST') &&
    $this->validateForm()) {
      $this->model_catalog_feedback->addfeedback($this->request
        ->post);
      $this->session->data['success'] = $this->language
        ->get('text_success');
      $url = '';
      if (isset($this->request->get['sort'])) {
        $url .='&sort=' . $this->request->get['sort'];}
      if (isset($this->request->get['order'])) {
```

```
        $url .='&order=' . $this->request->get['order'];}
      if (isset($this->request->get['page'])) {
        $url .='&page=' . $this->request->get['page'];
      }
      $this->redirect($this->url->link('catalog/feedback',
      'token=' . $this->session->data['token'] . $url, 'SSL'));
    }
  $this->getForm();
}
```

When you click on the **Insert** button, this function is called, and it loads the feedback language file and sets the title of the document as "Feedback", as `heading_feedback` holds the text "Feedback". Then, it loads the `feedback.php` model file and checks whether its form is submitted or not. If the form is not submitted, it will load the `getForm()` function from the same `feedback.php` controller file that shows the form. If the form is submitted and is validated, it will save the data into the database and sends the `$_POST` value to model `$this->model_catalog_feedback->addfeedback($this->request->post);` for adding the feedback to the database. Then, the success session is set and applied with the sort order and limit and is redirected to the list of the feedback.

```
public function update() {
  $this->language->load('catalog/feedback');
  $this->document->setTitle($this->language
    ->get('heading_feedback'));
  $this->load->model('catalog/feedback');
  if (($this->request->server['REQUEST_METHOD'] == 'POST') &&
    $this->validateForm()) {
    $this->model_catalog_feedback->editfeedback($this->request
      ->get['feedback_id'], $this->request->post);
    $this->session->data['success'] = $this->language
      ->get('text_success');
    $url = '';
    if (isset($this->request->get['sort'])) {
      $url .='&sort=' . $this->request->get['sort'];}
    if (isset($this->request->get['order'])) {
      $url .='&order=' . $this->request->get['order'];}
    if (isset($this->request->get['page'])) {
      $url .='&page=' . $this->request->get['page'];}
    $this->redirect($this->url->link('catalog/feedback', 'token='
      . $this->session->data['token'] . $url, 'SSL'));
  }
  $this->getForm();
}
```

When we click on the edit link, the update page is loaded and hence the update function of this controller is called. It also loads the `feedback.php` language file, sets the title of the document, and loads the `feedback.php` model file. If the submitted data are valid and the requested method is POST, the feedback will be saved into the database, else it again calls the form and the form is shown. Update is made using code `$this->model_catalog_feedback->editfeedback($this->request->get['feedback_id'], $this->request->post);`. It calls the `update` function of the feedback model, and the session is set, it is applied the sort order limit, and redirected to the list of the feedback.

```
public function delete() {
  $this->language->load('catalog/feedback');
  $this->document->setfeedback_author($this->language
    ->get('heading_feedback'));
  $this->load->model('catalog/feedback');
  if (isset($this->request->post['selected']) && $this
    ->validateDelete()) {
    foreach ($this->request->post['selected'] as $feedback_id) {
      $this->model_catalog_feedback->deletefeedback($feedback_id);
    }
    $this->session->data['success'] = $this->language
      ->get('text_success');
    $url = '';
    if (isset($this->request->get['sort'])) {
      $url .='&sort=' . $this->request->get['sort'];}
    if (isset($this->request->get['order'])) {
      $url .= '&order=' . $this->request->get['order'];
    }
    if (isset($this->request->get['page'])) {
      $url .='&page=' . $this->request->get['page'];
    }
    $this->redirect($this->url->link('catalog/feedback', 'token='
    . $this->session->data['token'] . $url, 'SSL'));
  }
  $this->getList();
}
```

For deleting the feedback, the preceding code is used. On the list of feedback page when you select the checkbox, which is to the left of each row, and click on the **delete** button, the delete function of the controller is executed. It deletes the selected rows from the database, and the query that it runs is with the help of `$this->model_catalog_feedback->deletefeedback($feedback_id);`. The `deletefeedback` function will be run on the loop or on each selected row, and the rows are deleted.

Till now, we have shown you the full code but taking the length of the code into consideration, we are now doing a copy, paste, and replace action by which it will be easy for us to mention only the required code and discard the one that is already mentioned.

Navigate to `admin/controller/catalog/information.php` and open it. Now find the protected function, `getList()`, copy the whole function to our `feedback.php` controller, and paste to the `controller` class just below the `delete` class as we mentioned previously; however, you can keep it anywhere outside the other functions. After pasting, find all the "information" words and change them to "feedback". Likewise, find all the "title" words and change them to `feedback_author` but only within the `getList()` function and not in the entire document. With the changes mentioned previously, you will see the following lines of code:

```
if (isset($this->request->get['sort'])) {
  $sort = $this->request->get['sort'];
} else {
  $sort = 'fd.feedback_author';
}
$url = '';
if (isset($this->request->get['sort'])) {
  $url .='&sort=' . $this->request->get['sort'];
}
```

Whenever you click on Sort Order on the list, it starts to order the table according to the sort order. If there is no click, it sorts by `feedback_author`. Similarly, the page number and order number are set as well as the get value of sort of the URL.

```
$this->data['breadcrumbs'] = array();
$this->data['breadcrumbs'][] = array(
  'text'      => $this->language->get('text_home'),
  'href'      => $this->url->link('common/home', 'token=' . $this
  ->session->data['token'], 'SSL'),
  'separator' => false
);
```

Breadcrumbs are created in an array and passed on to the template file.

```
$this->data['insert'] = $this->url
  ->link('catalog/feedback/insert', 'token=' . $this->session
  ->data['token'] . $url, 'SSL');

$this->data['delete'] = $this->url
  ->link('catalog/feedback/delete', 'token=' . $this->session
  ->data['token'] . $url, 'SSL');
```

Insert and delete links are created and passed on to the template file.

```
$data = array(
  'sort'  => $sort,
  'order' => $order,
  'start' => ($page - 1) * $this->config
    ->get('config_admin_limit'),
  'limit' => $this->config->get('config_admin_limit')
);
$feedback_total = $this->model_catalog_feedback
  ->getTotalfeedbacks();
$results = $this->model_catalog_feedback->getfeedbacks($data);
```

Results are received by querying the database.

```
foreach ($results as $result) {
  $action = array();
  $action[] = array(
    'text' => $this->language->get('text_edit'),
  'href' => $this->url->link('catalog/feedback/update', 'token=' .
    $this->session->data['token'] . '&feedback_id=' .
    $result['feedback_id'] . $url, 'SSL')
  );
  $this->data['feedbacks'][] = array(
    'feedback_id' => $result['feedback_id'],
    'feedback_author' => $result['feedback_author'],
    'sort_order'      => $result['sort_order'],
    'selected'        =>isset($this->request->post['selected'])
      &&in_array($result['feedback_id'], $this->request
      ->post['selected']),
    'action'          => $action
  );
}
```

Results received are combined to make it an array and passed to the template file.

```
$this->data['heading_feedback_author'] = $this->language
  ->get('heading_feedback_author');
$this->data['text_no_results'] = $this->language
  ->get('text_no_results');
```

Messages are retrieved from the language file and passed to the template file. Now again navigate to admin/controller/catalog/information.php, and open it to find the getForm() protected function and copy the whole function's code to our feedback.php controller. Paste this into the controller class just below the getlist() function as we mentioned previously, but you can keep it anywhere outside the other functions.

After pasting, find all the "information" words and change them to "feedback", and likewise find all the "title" words and change them to feedback_author, but only within the getForm() function and not in the entire document. As there are some extra fields, we have to remove the following code snippet:

```
if (isset($this->request->post['keyword'])) {
  $this->data['keyword'] = $this->request->post['keyword'];
} elseif (!empty($feedback_info)) {
  $this->data['keyword'] = $feedback_info['keyword'];
} else {$this->data['keyword'] = '';}

if (isset($this->request->post['bottom'])) {
  $this->data['bottom'] = $this->request->post['bottom'];
} elseif (!empty($feedback_info)) {
  $this->data['bottom'] = $feedback_info['bottom'];
} else {$this->data['bottom'] = 0;}
```

Once the replacement is complete and the extra fields are removed, our getForm function is ready.

```
$this->data['heading_feedback_author'] = $this->language-
>get('heading_feedback_author');
$this->data['text_default'] = $this->language->get('text_default');
$this->data['text_enabled'] = $this->language->get('text_enabled');
```

The preceding lines of code, and many such lines in the function, take the text or the sentence from the language and pass it to the template files.

```
if (isset($this->request->get['feedback_id'])) && ($this->request
  ->server['REQUEST_METHOD'] != 'POST')) {
  $feedback_info = $this->model_catalog_feedback
    ->getfeedback($this->request->get['feedback_id']);
}
```

This part of code checks whether the feedback_id is passed with the GET method of the form, and if so, it will retrieve the feedback and assign it to $feedback_info.

```
$this->data['token'] = $this->session->data['token'];
```

To preserve the session state within the admin section, the token session is defined and needs to be passed within all the URLs used within the admin section.

```
$this->load->model('localisation/language');
$this->data['languages'] = $this->model_localisation_language
  ->getLanguages();
```

It loads the `language.php` model, which is at the localization folder on the model section. It is loaded to load languages used in the site. All languages used are passed to the template file as the languages variable.

```
if (isset($this->request->post['feedback_description'])) {
  $this->data['feedback_description'] = $this->request
    ->post['feedback_description'];
} elseif (isset($this->request->get['feedback_id'])) {
  $this->data['feedback_description'] = $this
    ->model_catalog_feedback->getfeedbackDescriptions($this
    ->request->get['feedback_id']);
} else {$this->data['feedback_description'] = array();}
```

The preceding code checks whether `feedback_description` is passed as POST, and `feedback_id` is passed as a GET method or something else. If `feedback_description` is passed as POST, it will hold the POST data and if `feedback_id` is passed as the GET method, it will retrieve `feedback_description` from the database. If it is none, it will assign the blank array to `feedback_description`.

```
$this->load->model('setting/store');
$this->data['stores'] = $this->model_setting_store->getStores();
```

It loads the `store.php` model from the setting folder and retrieves all the stores and passes it to the template as the stores variable.

```
if (isset($this->request->post['feedback_store'])) {
  $this->data['feedback_store'] = $this->request
    ->post['feedback_store'];
} elseif (isset($this->request->get['feedback_id'])) {
  $this->data['feedback_store'] = $this->model_catalog_feedback
    ->getfeedbackStores($this->request->get['feedback_id']);
} else {$this->data['feedback_store'] = array(0);}
```

If the store is passed as POST, it will hold the POST data; if `feedback_id` is passed as GET, it will retrieve the store from the database. If it is none, it will assign an array with the zero value to the store, which is the default store value. The overall request data is checked with the following lines of code.

```
if (isset($this->request->post['feedback_layout'])) {
  $this->data['feedback_layout'] = $this->request
  ->post['feedback_layout'];
} elseif (isset($this->request->get['feedback_id'])) {
  $this->data['feedback_layout'] = $this->model_catalog_feedback
  ->getfeedbackLayouts($this->request->get['feedback_id']);
} else {$this->data['feedback_layout'] = array();}
```

The code snippets check whether `feedback_layout` is passed as POST, `feedback_id` is passed as a GET method, or something else. If `feedback_layout` is passed as POST, it will hold the POST data, if `feedback_id` is passed as the GET, it will retrieve `feedback_layout` from the database. If it is none, it will assign the blank array to `feedback_layout`.

```
protected function validateForm() {
    if (!$this->user->hasPermission('modify', 'catalog/feedback')) {
        $this->error['warning'] = $this->language
          ->get('error_permission');
    }
    if ($this->error && !isset($this->error['warning'])) {
        $this->error['warning'] = $this->language
          ->get('error_warning');
    }
    if (!$this->error) {return true;} else {return false;}
}
```

The `validateForm()` function is to validate the form and needs to be copied just below the `getForm()` function. It checks for user permission, whether to modify the feedback section or not. If it does not have permission, an error is shown.

```
protected function validateDelete() {
    if (!$this->user->hasPermission('modify', 'catalog/feedback')) {
        $this->error['warning'] = $this->language
          ->get('error_permission');
    }
    if (!$this->error) {return true;} else {return false;}
}
```

The `validateDelete()` function is used to validate deletion. First, it checks whether the user has permission to modify or not. If the user has permission to modify, only he/she is able to delete. Then, they place the closing curly brace at the end for the class.

Creating the template files for form and list at the admin

Navigate to `admin/view/template/catalog/`, copy `information_form.tpl`, paste it in the same folder, and rename it as `feedback_form.tpl`. Likewise, copy the `information_list.tpl` file, paste on the same folder, and rename it to `feedback_list.tpl`.

Now open the `feedback_list.tpl` file, look for `information`, and replace all with `feedback`. Likewise, look for `title` and replace all with `feedback_author`. Your `feedback_list.tpl` is now ready after the replacing process. Most of the code is already described in the `feedback_list.tpl` file, so we are ignoring them.

Now open the `feedback_form.tpl` file, look for `information`, and replace all with `feedback`. Likewise, find `title` and replace all with `feedback_author`. It contains some extra fields, so we have to remove them. Remove the following code from the `feedback_form.tpl` file:

```
<tr>
  <td><?php echo $entry_keyword; ?></td>
  <td><input type="text" name="keyword" value="<?php echo
    $keyword; ?>" /></td>
</tr><tr>
  <td><?php echo $entry_bottom; ?></td>
  <td><?php if ($bottom) { ?> <input type="checkbox" name="bottom"
    value="1" checked="checked" />
  <?php } else { ?> <input type="checkbox" name="bottom" value="1"
     />
  <?php } ?></td>
</tr><tr>
<td><?php echo $entry_keyword; ?></td>
<td><input type="text" name="keyword" value="<?php echo $keyword;
  ?>" /></td>
</tr><tr>
  <td><?php echo $entry_bottom; ?></td>
  <td><?php if ($bottom) { ?> <input type="checkbox" name="bottom"
    value="1" checked="checked" />
  <?php } else { ?> <input type="checkbox" name="bottom" value="1"
     />
  <?php } ?></td>
</tr>
```

After removing the preceding code, `feedback_form.tpl` is ready. We are describing some code snippets from the `feedback_form.tpl` file, while the others are described already.

```
<td><textarea name="feedback_description[<?php echo
  $language['language_id']; ?>][description]" id="description<?php
    echo $language['language_id']; ?>"><?php echo
    isset($feedback_description[$language['language_id']]) ?
    $feedback_description[$language['language_id']]['description']
    : ''; ?></textarea>
  <?php if (isset($error_description[$language['language_id']])) {
    ?>
```

```
    <span class="error"><?php echo
      $error_description[$language['language_id']]; ?></span>
    <?php } ?>
  </td>
```

The preceding code shows the text area. Here the name of the text area of the form is named as the `feedback_description[<?php echo $language['language_id']; ?>][description]` array for storing description as per the language. To show the editor, `id=description<?php echo $language['language_id']; ?>` plays a vital role. With the same ID name, the following code is called to show the editor:

```
<script type="text/javascript"
  src="view/javascript/ckeditor/ckeditor.js"></script>
<script type="text/javascript"><!--
<?phpforeach ($languages as $language) { ?>
CKEDITOR.replace('description<?php echo $language['language_id'];
  ?>', {
  filebrowserBrowseUrl:
    'index.php?route=common/filemanager&token=<?php echo $token;
    ?>',
  filebrowserImageBrowseUrl:
    'index.php?route=common/filemanager&token=<?php echo $token;
    ?>',
  filebrowserFlashBrowseUrl:
    'index.php?route=common/filemanager&token=<?php echo $token;
    ?>',
  filebrowserUploadUrl:
    'index.php?route=common/filemanager&token=<?php echo $token;
    ?>',
  filebrowserImageUploadUrl:
    'index.php?route=common/filemanager&token=<?php echo $token;
    ?>',
  filebrowserFlashUploadUrl:
    'index.php?route=common/filemanager&token=<?php echo $token;
    ?>'
});
<?php } ?>
//--></script>
```

With this, the JavaScript code CKEditor is loaded on the text area field. Write the entire code and call the ID of the text area at `CKEDITOR. replace('description<?php echo $language['language_id']; ?>'`, replace with your ID of the text area, and the editor will be shown at your text area.

With this, we complete the changes at the admin section. Now we are moving towards the frontend or catalog folder.

Creating the model file at the catalog folder frontend

We need to create a model file to retrieve data from the database. We will make the file at the catalog folder. Navigate to `catalog/model/catalog/` and create `feedback.php` and insert the following lines of code:

```php
<?php
Class ModelCatalogFeedback extends Model {
  public function getFeedbacks() {
    $query = $this->db->query("SELECT DISTINCT * FROM " .
      DB_PREFIX. "feedback f LEFT JOIN " . DB_PREFIX
      ."feedback_description fd ON (f.feedback_id =
      fd.feedback_id) LEFT JOIN " . DB_PREFIX. "feedback_to_store
      f2s ON (f.feedback_id = f2s.feedback_id)WHERE fd.language_id
      = '" . (int)$this->config->get('config_language_id') . "'
      AND f2s.store_id = '" . (int)$this->config
      ->get('config_store_id') . "' AND f.status = '1'");

    return $query->rows;
  }
  public function getTotalFeedbacks() {
    $query = $this->db->query("SELECT COUNT(*) AS total FROM " .
      DB_PREFIX . "feedback f LEFT JOIN " . DB_PREFIX .
      "feedback_to_store f2s ON (f.feedback_id = f2s.feedback_id)
      WHERE f2s.store_id = '" . (int)$this->config
      ->get('config_store_id') . "' AND f.status = '1'");

    return $query->row['total'];
  }
}
?>
```

We create a class named `ModelCatalogFeedback` as the `feedback.php` file is created in the catalog folder. Then, we create a public function, `getFeedbacks`. It queries the database to select all the data that have the status of 1 from the `feedback` table and the `feedback_description` table, which is then returned. At last, we create a public function called `getTotalFeedbacks`. It queries the database and counts all the active feedback. It returns the total number of active feedback. The model file, `feedback.php`, is ready.

Creating the language file at the frontend

Now navigate to `catalog/language/english/product/`, create a `feedback.php` file, and paste the following lines of code:

```php
<?php
$_['text_feedback']       = 'List of feedback';
$_['text_description']    = 'List of feedback';
$_['text_keywords']    = 'List of feedback';
$_['text_error']          = 'Feedback not found!';
$_['text_empty']          = 'There are no feedbacks to list.';
?>
```

The required sentences are defined on the variable. Create the `feedback.php` language file.

Creating the controller file at the frontend

After creating the language and model file, we are creating the controller file. Navigate to `catalog/controller/product/`, create `feedback.php`, and insert the following code:

```php
<?php
class ControllerProductFeedback extends Controller {
  public function index() {
    $this->language->load('product/feedback');
    $this->load->model('catalog/feedback');
```

The language file and model files are loaded to get the language and retrieve the model methods.

```php
if (isset($this->request->get['page'])) {
  $page = $this->request->get['page'];
  } else { $page = 1;}
if (isset($this->request->get['limit'])) {
  $limit = $this->request->get['limit'];
  } else {
  $limit = $this->config->get('config_catalog_limit');
  }
```

It will set the $page variable to the GET value of the page if GET is set, else $page will be 1. This is needed for pagination. It will set the $limit variable to the GET value of the limit. If GET is not set, $limit will be the value of the catalog limit of the setting from the admin.

```
$this->data['breadcrumbs'] = array();
$this->data['breadcrumbs'][] = array(
   'text'       => $this->language->get('text_home'),
   'href'       => $this->url->link('common/home'),
   'separator' => false
);
$this->data['breadcrumbs'][] = array(
   'text'       => $this->language->get('text_feedback'),
   'href'       => $this->url->link('product/feedback'),
   'separator' =>'::'
);
```

It adds the breadcrumb, which is passed as an array to the template file.

```
$this->document->setTitle($this->language
   ->get('text_feedback'));
$this->document->setDescription($this->language
   ->get('text_description'));
$this->document->setKeywords($this->language
   ->get('text_keywords'));
```

The preceding lines of code set the document title, metadescription, and keywords. These are described in the language file.

```
$this->data['heading_title'] = $this->language
   ->get('text_feedback');
$this->data['text_empty'] = $this->language
   ->get('text_empty');
$this->data['button_continue'] = $this->language
   ->get('button_continue');
```

The preceding lines of code are for retrieving the message from the language file and passing it to the template file.

```
$url = '';
if (isset($this->request->get['page'])) {
   $url .='&page=' . $this->request->get['page'];
}
$this->data['feedbacks'] = array();
$data = array(
   'start'                 => ($page - 1) * $limit,
   'limit'                 => $limit
);
```

The `$data` variable is passed as the parameter to retrieve only a limited number of the feedback data.

```
$results = $this->model_catalog_feedback->getfeedbacks($data);
foreach ($results as $result) {
  $this->data['feedbacks'][] = array(
    'feedback_author'  => $result['feedback_author'],
     'description'=>html_entity_decode($result['description'],
      ENT_QUOTES, 'UTF-8'),
  );
}
```

The `$results` variable retrieves the data, and it is run through the loop to assign only the author's name and the described feedback. Feedback description is stored as encoded HTML, and we have to decode it to show only the formatted HTML; we parse it with `html_entity_decode`.

```
$feedback_total = $this->model_catalog_feedback
  ->getTotalFeedbacks();
```

The preceding line of code retrieves the total number of active feedback.

```
$pagination = new Pagination();
$pagination->total = $feedback_total;
$pagination->page = $page;
$pagination->limit = $limit;
$pagination->text = $this->language->get('text_pagination');
$pagination->url = $this->url
  ->link('product/feedback','&page={page}');
$this->data['pagination'] = $pagination->render();
```

The preceding lines of code pass the pagination variable to the template file to show pagination.

```
$this->data['limit'] = $limit;
$this->data['continue'] = $this->url->link('common/home');

if (file_exists(DIR_TEMPLATE . $this->config
  ->get('config_template') . '/template/product/feedback.tpl')) {
    $this->template = $this->config->get('config_template') .
    '/template/product/feedback.tpl';
  } else {
    $this->template = 'default/template/product/feedback.tpl';
  }
```

It checks whether the template file for the current active theme is available or not, and if available, it will render the `feedback.tpl` file, else it renders the `feedback.tpl` file from the default theme.

```
$this->children = array(
   'common/column_left',
   'common/column_right',
   'common/content_top',
   'common/content_bottom',
   'common/footer',
   'common/header'
);
$this->response->setOutput($this->render());
}
}
?>
```

With this, the `feedback.php` controller file is also ready.

Creating the template file at the frontend

Navigate to `catalog/view/theme/default/template/product`, create `feedback.tpl`, and insert the following code:

```
<?php echo $header; ?><?php echo $column_left; ?><?php echo
   $column_right; ?>
<div id="content"><?php echo $content_top; ?>
<div class="breadcrumb">
<?phpforeach ($breadcrumbs as $breadcrumb) { ?>
<?php echo $breadcrumb['separator']; ?><a href="<?php echo
  $breadcrumb['href']; ?>"><?php echo $breadcrumb['text']; ?></a>
<?php } ?>
</div>
```

The preceding lines of code show the breadcrumbs.

```
<h1><?php echo $heading_title; ?></h1>
<?php if ($feedbacks) { ?>
<div class="content">
<?phpforeach ($feedbacks as $feedback) { ?>
<div>
<div class="name">Name: <?php echo $feedback['feedback_author']; ?></
div>
<div class="description"><?php echo $feedback['description']; ?></div>
</div>
<?php } ?>
```

The preceding lines of code show the **List of feedback**, **Author name**, and its **description** as shown in the following screenshot:

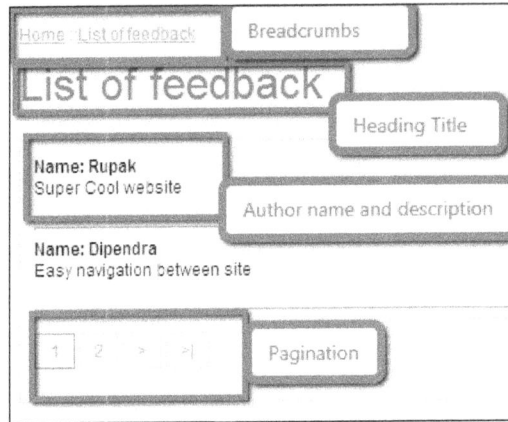

To show the pagination for the template file, we have to insert the following lines of code to the part where we would like to show the pagination:

```
<div class="pagination"><?php echo $pagination; ?></div>
```

It shows the pagination in the template file and mostly we show the pagination at the bottom, so paste the code at the end of the feedback.tpl file.

```
</div>
<?php } ?>
<?php if (!$feedbacks) { ?>
<div class="content"><?php echo $text_empty; ?></div>
```

If there are no feedback, a message saying **There are no feedbacks to show** is shown as per the language file.

```
<div class="buttons">
<div class="right"><a href="<?php echo $continue; ?>"
class="button"><?php echo $button_continue; ?></a></div>
</div>
<?php } ?>
<?php echo $content_bottom; ?></div>
<?php echo $footer; ?>
```

With this, the template file is also complete and thus our feedback management is complete.

Now, we insert the link on the menu to be able to manage the feedback, so navigate to `admin/language/english/common/header.php` and look for the following line of code:

```
$_['text_zone']                          = 'Zones';
```

And after this insert the following line of code:

```
$_['text_feedback']                        = 'Feedback';
```

In the language file, we defined `text_feedback`, which we need to call at the controller and pass it to the template. Now, we are calling in the controller file, so navigate to `admin/controller/common/header.php` and look for the following line of code:

```
$this->data['heading_title'] = $this->language->get('heading_title');
```

Then insert the following line of code:

```
$this->data['text_feedback'] = $this->language->get(' text_feedback');
```

Likewise, for linking the Feedback word, we have to define the URL and it is done as shown in the following code. For this, we have to insert the following lines of code just before `$this->data['stores'] = array();`:

```
$this->data['feedback_link'] = $this->url->link('catalog/feedback',
'token=' . $this->session->data['token'], 'SSL');
```

Now navigate to `admin/view/template/common/header.tpl` and look for the following line of code:

```
<li><a href="<?php echo $review; ?>"><?php echo $text_review; ?></a></
li>
```

Then, insert the following line of code:

```
<li><a href="<?php echo $feedback; ?>"><?php echo $feedback; ?></a></
li>
```

With the preceding code insertion, you will be able to see the Feedback link when you hover on Catalog of the admin menu. Now click on the Feedback link and you will be able to see the list of feedback, if there is any, as well as the **Insert** button and the **Delete** button. Now you are ready to manage the feedback.

Till now we have created the page to list the feedback and a form to edit, delete, and insert the feedback. Now, you can also create the module for feedback by following the steps in the previous chapters. For viewing the list of feedback at the frontend, we have to use the link as follows and insert the link somewhere in the templates so that visitors will be able to see the feedback list.

```
http://www.example.com/index.php?route=product/feedback
```

The Tips module

We are creating the Tips module. When the Tips module is activated at the admin section from **Admin | Extensions | Order Totals**, it will be listed in the Order Totals listing page, and you will see the Tips module activated at Shopping Cart. After entering the amount and clicking on the **Apply Tips** button, the extra amount is added to the order total, which adds to the total cost of the order.

Creating the language file at the admin section

To create a language file for the Order Total module, we have to create the file at the total folder in the language folder. Navigate to `admin/language/english/total/`, and create a `tips.php` file and insert the following lines of code:

```php
<?php
$_['heading_title']    = 'Tips Fee';
$_['text_total']       = 'Order Totals';
$_['text_success'] = 'Success: You have modified tips fee total!';
$_['entry_total']      = 'Order Total:';
$_['entry_fee']        = 'Fee:';
$_['entry_tax_class']  = 'Tax Class:';
$_['entry_status']     = 'Status:';
$_['entry_sort_order'] = 'Sort Order:';
$_['error_permission'] = 'Warning: You do not have permission to
modify Tips fee total!';
?>
```

Creating the controller file at the admin section

After creating the language file, we now need to create the controller file. Navigate to `admin/controller/total/` and create `tips.php` and insert the following code. Most of the code has already been described, so we will skip the descriptions here.

```php
<?php
class ControllerTotaltips extends Controller {
  private $error = array();
  public function index() {
    $this->language->load('total/tips');
    $this->document->setTitle($this->language
      ->get('heading_title'));
    $this->load->model('setting/setting');
    if (($this->request->server['REQUEST_METHOD'] == 'POST') &&
    $this->validate()) {
      $this->model_setting_setting->editSetting('tips', $this
        ->request->post);
      $this->session->data['success'] = $this->language
        ->get('text_success');
      $this->redirect($this->url->link('extension/total', 'token='
      . $this->session->data['token'], 'SSL'));
    }
```

The `group` column in the database `setting` table has the value `tips` as the word "tips" is passed from `$this->model_setting_setting->editSetting('tips', $this->request->post);` and therefore each setting value of the Tips module will have the `tips` value in the `group` column. When saved, we will see rows at the setting table as shown in the following screenshot:

	setting_id	store_id	group	key	value	serialized
ete	272	0	tips	tips_sort_order		0
ete	271	0	tips	tips_status	1	0

The following is the language section part in the controller to assign the variable, which will be used on the template files:

```
$this->data['heading_title'] = $this->language
  ->get('heading_title');
$this->data['text_enabled'] = $this->language
  ->get('text_enabled');
$this->data['text_disabled'] = $this->language
  ->get('text_disabled');
$this->data['text_none'] = $this->language->get('text_none');
$this->data['entry_status'] = $this->language
  ->get('entry_status');
$this->data['entry_sort_order'] = $this->language
  ->get('entry_sort_order');
$this->data['button_save'] = $this->language->get('button_save');
$this->data['button_cancel'] = $this->language
  ->get('button_cancel');

if (isset($this->error['warning'])) {
  $this->data['error_warning'] = $this->error['warning'];
} else {
  $this->data['error_warning'] = '';
}
```

Up to this point, the language is loaded to the variable and passed to the template files.

```
$this->data['breadcrumbs'] = array();
$this->data['breadcrumbs'][] = array(
  'text'      => $this->language->get('text_home'),
  'href'      => $this->url->link('common/home', 'token=' . $this
    ->session->data['token'], 'SSL'),
  'separator' => false
);
```

```
$this->data['breadcrumbs'][] = array(
   'text'      => $this->language->get('text_total'),
   'href'      => $this->url->link('extension/total', 'token=' .
     $this->session->data['token'], 'SSL'),
   'separator' =>' :: '
);
$this->data['breadcrumbs'][] = array(
   'text'      => $this->language->get('heading_title'),
   'href'      => $this->url->link('total/tips', 'token=' . $this
     ->session->data['token'], 'SSL'),
   'separator' =>' :: '
);
```

Breadcrumbs are created in an array and passed to the template files.

```
$this->data['action'] = $this->url->link('total/tips', 'token=' .
  $this->session->data['token'], 'SSL');
$this->data['cancel'] = $this->url->link('extension/total',
  'token=' . $this->session->data['token'], 'SSL');

if (isset($this->request->post['tips_status'])) {
  $this->data['tips_status'] = $this->request
    ->post['tips_status'];
} else {
  $this->data['tips_status'] = $this->config->get('tips_status');
}
if (isset($this->request->post['tips_sort_order'])) {
  $this->data['tips_sort_order'] = $this->request
    ->post['tips_sort_order'];
} else {
  $this->data['tips_sort_order'] = $this->config
    ->get('tips_sort_order');
}
$this->template = 'total/tips.tpl';
$this->children = array(
  'common/header',
  'common/footer'
);
$this->response->setOutput($this->render());
}

protected function validate() {
  if (!$this->user->hasPermission('modify', 'total/tips')) {
    $this->error['warning'] = $this->language
      ->get('error_permission');
  }
```

```
if (!$this->error) {
  return true;
} else {
  return false;
}
}
}
?>
```

Until here, the cancel and form action URL are defined, and the status of the Tips module is assigned as per the active POST method, else from the database config settings. Likewise, a sort order of the Tips module is assigned and the tips.tpl template is rendered.

The validate function is to check whether the user has the permission to modify or not. If they do, only then it returns true, else false.

Creating the template file at the admin section

Navigate to admin/view/template/total/ and create tips.tpl and insert the following code:

```
<?php echo $header; ?>
<div id="content">
<div class="breadcrumb">
<?php foreach ($breadcrumbs as $breadcrumb) { ?>
<?php echo $breadcrumb['separator']; ?><a href="<?php echo
  $breadcrumb['href']; ?>"><?php echo $breadcrumb['text']; ?></a>
<?php } ?>
</div>
<?php if ($error_warning) { ?>
<div class="warning"><?php echo $error_warning; ?></div>
<?php } ?>
<div class="box">
<div class="heading">
<h1><imgsrc="view/image/total.png" alt="" /><?php echo $heading_title;
?></h1>
<div class="buttons"><a onclick="$('#form').submit();"
class="button"><?php echo $button_save; ?></a><a href="<?php echo
  $cancel; ?>" class="button"><?php echo $button_cancel; ?></a></div>
</div>
<div class="content">
<form action="<?php echo $action; ?>" method="post"
enctype="multipart/form-data" id="form">
```

```
<table class="form">
<tr>
<td><?php echo $entry_status; ?></td>
<td><select name="tips_status">
<?php if ($tips_status) { ?>
<option value="1" selected="selected"><?php echo $text_enabled; ?></
option>
<option value="0"><?php echo $text_disabled; ?></option>
<?php } else { ?>
<option value="1"><?php echo $text_enabled; ?></option>
<option value="0" selected="selected"><?php echo $text_disabled; ?></
option>
<?php } ?>
</select></td>
</tr>
<tr>
<td><?php echo $entry_sort_order; ?></td>
<td><input type="text" name="tips_sort_order" value="<?php echo $tips_
sort_order; ?>" size="1" /></td>
</tr>
</table>
</form>
</div>
</div>
</div>
<?php echo $footer; ?>
```

Changes made in the cart file at the frontend

Navigate to `catalog/view/theme/default/template/checkout/` and open `cart. tpl` and paste the following code just before the `<?php if ($voucher_status) { ?>` code.

```
<?php if ($this->config->get('tips_status')==1) { ?>
<tr class="highlight">
<td><?php if ($next == 'tips') { ?>
<input type="radio" name="next" value="tips" id="use_tips"
  checked="checked" />
    <?php } else { ?>
<input type="radio" name="next" value="tips" id="use_tips" />
<?php } ?></td>
<td>Enter the Tips</td>
</tr>
<?php } ?>
```

The preceding code will show a radio button followed by the **Enter the Tips** text. On selecting this radio button, div with the id of `tips` is displayed.

Now just before the `<div id="voucher" class="content">` line, paste the following code:

```
<div id="tips" class="content" style="display: <?php echo ($next
  == 'tips' ? 'block' : 'none'); ?>;">
<form action="<?php echo $action; ?>" method="post"
  enctype="multipart/form-data">
      Enter your amount 
<input type="text" name="tips" value="" />
<input type="hidden" name="next" value="tips" />
 
<input type="submit" value="Apply Tips" class="button" />
</form>
</div>
```

It shows the **Enter your amount** form and an **Apply Tips** button.

Changes in the shopping cart page to show tips

Navigate to `catalog/controller/checkout/` and open `cart.php`. Look for `// Voucher` and paste the following lines of code before it:

```
// Tips
if (isset($this->request->post['tips'])) {
  $this->session->data['tips'] = $this->request->post['tips'];
  $this->session->data['success'] = $this->language
    ->get('text_tips');
  $this->redirect($this->url->link('checkout/cart'));
}
```

It activates the session for total extension. While installing the Order Total module, it is saved on the extension table as total just like the Tips module gets saved as shown in the following screenshot:

extension_id	type	code
429	total	tips

So once the session of tips is activated, the entire total is calculated and we do not need to work out another. We just need to activate the session of the tips, which we have done with the preceding code. With this, our Order Total module is complete.

Summary

In this chapter, we learned the ways to manage data. This was achieved by creating pages, listing it out, inserting the data to the database and retrieving it either to display or to edit, and finally deleting the data. Likewise, we showed you how to list the data at the frontend by making the page. At the end, we created the Order Total Tips module and showed you how it changed the order totals. Using this, you will be able to create modules and pages to manage the data across OpenCart.

Index

[PACKT] open source
PUBLISHING
community experience distilled

Thank you for buying
Getting started with OpenCart Module Development

About Packt Publishing

Packt, pronounced 'packed', published its first book "*Mastering phpMyAdmin for Effective MySQL Management*" in April 2004 and subsequently continued to specialize in publishing highly focused books on specific technologies and solutions.

Our books and publications share the experiences of your fellow IT professionals in adapting and customizing today's systems, applications, and frameworks. Our solution based books give you the knowledge and power to customize the software and technologies you're using to get the job done. Packt books are more specific and less general than the IT books you have seen in the past. Our unique business model allows us to bring you more focused information, giving you more of what you need to know, and less of what you don't.

Packt is a modern, yet unique publishing company, which focuses on producing quality, cutting-edge books for communities of developers, administrators, and newbies alike. For more information, please visit our website: www.packtpub.com.

About Packt Open Source

In 2010, Packt launched two new brands, Packt Open Source and Packt Enterprise, in order to continue its focus on specialization. This book is part of the Packt Open Source brand, home to books published on software built around Open Source licences, and offering information to anybody from advanced developers to budding web designers. The Open Source brand also runs Packt's Open Source Royalty Scheme, by which Packt gives a royalty to each Open Source project about whose software a book is sold.

Writing for Packt

We welcome all inquiries from people who are interested in authoring. Book proposals should be sent to author@packtpub.com. If your book idea is still at an early stage and you would like to discuss it first before writing a formal book proposal, contact us; one of our commissioning editors will get in touch with you.

We're not just looking for published authors; if you have strong technical skills but no writing experience, our experienced editors can help you develop a writing career, or simply get some additional reward for your expertise.

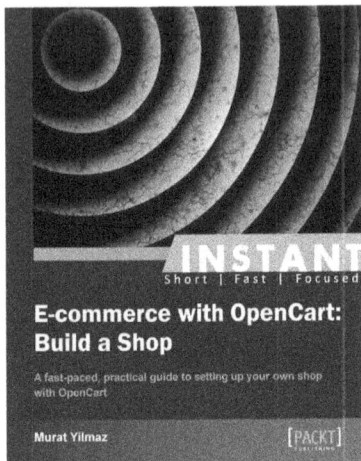

Instant E-commerce with OpenCart: Build a Shop [Instant]

ISBN: 978-1-78216-968-0   Paperback: 70 pages

A fast-paced, practical guide to setting up your own shop with OpenCart

1. Learn something new in an Instant! A short, fast, focused guide delivering immediate results

2. Install and configure OpenCart correctly

3. Tackle difficult tasks such as payment gateways, shipping options, product attributes, and managing orders

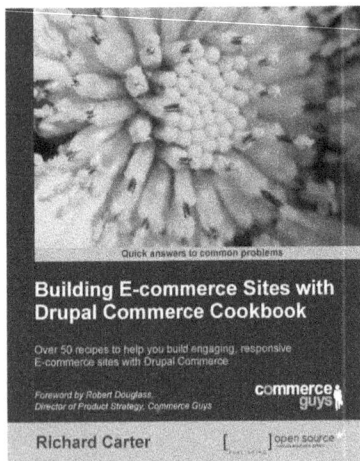

E-commerce with OpenCart: Build a Shop

INSTANT
Short | Fast | Focused

A fast-paced, practical guide to setting up your own shop with OpenCart

Murat Yilmaz   [PACKT]

Spring Python 1.1

ISBN: 978-1-78216-122-6   Paperback: 206 pages

Over 50 recipes to help you build engaging, responsive E-commerce sites with Drupal Commerce

1. Learn how to build attractive eCommerce sites with Drupal Commerce

2. Customise your Drupal Commerce store for maximum impact

3. Reviewed by the creators of Drupal Commerce: The CommerceGuys

Building E-commerce Sites with Drupal Commerce Cookbook

Quick answers to common problems

Over 50 recipes to help you build engaging, responsive E-commerce sites with Drupal Commerce

Foreword by Robert Douglass, Director of Product Strategy, Commerce Guys

commerce guys

Richard Carter   [   ] open source

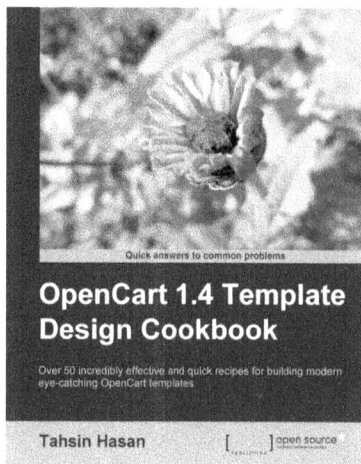

OpenCart 1.4 Template Design Cookbook

ISBN: 978-1-84951-430-9   Paperback: 328 pages

Over 50 incredibly effective and quick recipes for building modern eye-catching OpenCart templates

1. Customize dynamic menus, logos, headers, footers, and every other section using tricks you won't find in the official documentation

2. A great mix of recipes for beginners, intermediate, and advanced OpenCart template designers

3. Develop and customize dynamic, powerful OpenCart templates to make your website stand out from the crowd

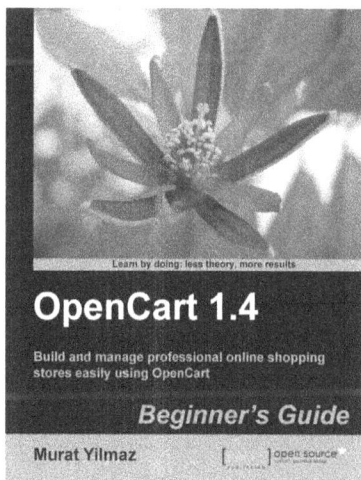

OpenCart 1.4: Beginner's Guide

ISBN: 978-1-84951-302-9   Paperback: 240 pages

Build and mange professional online shopping stores easily using OpenCart

1. Develop a professional, easy-to-use, attractive online store and shopping cart solution using OpenCart that meets today's modern e-commerce standards

2. Easily integrate your online store with one of the more popular payment gateways like PayPal and shipping methods such as UPS and USPS

3. Provide coupon codes, discounts, and wholesale options for your customers to increase demand on your online store

Please check **www.PacktPub.com** for information on our titles